CANAL HOUSE
COOKING

CANAL HOUSE
No. 6 Coryell Street
Lambertville, NJ 08530
thecanalhouse.com

ISBN 978-0-9827394-1-9

Printed in China

Book design by CANAL HOUSE, a group of artists who collaborate on design projects.
This book was designed by Melissa Hamilton, Christopher Hirsheimer & Teresa Hopkins.
Edited by Margo True & Copyedited by Valerie Saint-Rossy.
Editorial assistance by Julie Sproesser

Distributed to the trade by
Andrews McMeel Publishing, LLC
an Andrews McMeel Universal company
1130 Walnut Street, Kansas City, Missouri 64106

www.andrewsmcmeel.com

11 12 13 14 OGP 10 9 8 7 6 5 4 3 2

ATTENTION: SCHOOLS AND BUSINESSES
Andrews McMeel books are available at quantity discounts with bulk purchase for
educational, business, or sales promotional use. For information, please e-mail
the Andrews McMeel Publishing Special Sales Department:
specialsales@amuniversal.com

CANAL HOUSE
COOKING

Volume N° 5

Hamilton & Hirsheimer

Welcome to Canal House—our studio, workshop, dining room, office, kitchen, and atelier devoted to good ideas and good work relating to the world of food. We write, photograph, design, and paint, but in our hearts we both think of ourselves as cooks first.

Our loft studio is in an old red brick warehouse. A beautiful lazy canal runs alongside the building. We have a simple galley kitchen. Two small apartment-size stoves sit snugly side by side against a white tiled wall. We have a dishwasher, but prefer to hand wash the dishes so we can look out of the tall window next to the sink and see the ducks swimming in the canal or watch the raindrops splashing into the water.

And every day we cook. Starting in the morning we tell each other what we made for dinner the night before. Midday, we stop our work, set the table simply with paper napkins, and have lunch. We cook seasonally because that's what makes sense. So it came naturally to write down what we cook. The recipes in our books are what we make for ourselves and our families all year long. If you cook your way through a few, you'll see that who we are comes right through in the pages: that we are crazy for tomatoes in summer, make braises and stews all fall, and turn oranges into marmalade in winter.

Canal House Cooking is home cooking by home cooks for home cooks. We use ingredients found in most markets. All the recipes are easy to prepare for the novice and experienced cook alike. We want to share them with you as fellow cooks along with our love of food and all its rituals. The everyday practice of simple cooking and the enjoyment of eating are two of the greatest pleasures in life.

CHRISTOPHER HIRSHEIMER served as food and design editor for *Metropolitan Home* magazine, and was one of the founders of *Saveur* magazine, where she was executive editor. She is a writer and a photographer.

MELISSA HAMILTON cofounded the restaurant Hamilton's Grill Room in Lambertville, New Jersey, where she served as executive chef. She worked at *Martha Stewart Living, Cook's Illustrated,* and at *Saveur* as the food editor.

Christopher and Melissa in the Canal House kitchen

It's Always Five O'Clock Somewhere
christmas eve by gabrielle hamilton 8
grower champagnes by frank stitt 13

Wørking Up an Appetite
an appetizing smørrebrød 20
fried oysters 26, escargots sans their shells 26

Big Livers
goose liver & pork terrine 30, goose liver pâté with truffles 33
toast points 33, foie gras au torchon 35, brioche toasts 35
seared foie gras with green grapes 36

Uova Huevos Oeufs Eggs
scrambled eggs with truffles 40, piquillo pepper eggs 40
pimentón fried eggs 43, eggs with caper & parsley butter sauce 43

Crêpes
broiled pig's feet crêpes 46, crêpes 47
buckwheat crêpes 49, lemon sugar crêpes 49, orange sugar crêpes 49
chocolate & toasted hazelnut crêpes 49, pear & gorgonzola crêpes 49
buckwheat blini with smoked salmon & trout roe 50

Grandma's Gnocchi
our imaginary grandmother's gnocchi 54, turkey neck sugo 56
simplest tomato sauce 57, simple tomato-pancetta sauce 57
truffled lobster with gnocchi 58, whole pot-roasted chicken with gnocchi 60
green & white soup with gnocchi 61

Eat Your Vegetables

niloufer's cauliflower & chickpeas 64
the apple farm's roasted cauliflower 65, warm savoy cabbage salad 65
red cabbage with apples & chestnuts 66
puréed celery root & potatoes 68
collards & bacon 69, cauliflower soufflé 71

Fins 'n' Things

sole & shrimp 74, lobster with browned cream 76
steamed mussels with potatoes 77, chowder 79

Sausages

making fresh sausages 82, italian sausage 83, duck sausage with quatre épices 85
lamb sausage with currants 85, sausages with apples & onions 88
grilled sausages & quail 89, polenta 89, cassoulet our way 91, confit of goose legs 91

Big Beautiful Birds

roast goose with ten legs 94, apples cooked with cumin 95
chicken & mushrooms 96, truffled chicken 99

Serious Meat

fresh ham with madeira sauce 102, roasted pork belly 106, céléri rémoulade 106
moroccan lamb roast 107, mint sauce 107, braised beef with currants & caraway 108

Holiday Sweets

sugar cookies 112, coconut cookies 113
lemon cookies 113, nut cookies 113, orange-rosemary cookies 113
oeufs à la neige 117, pets de nonnes 118, pear upside-down cake 121, apple fritters 122

OUR OPEN DOOR POLICY

ONE MORNING A THICK ICY VELVET COVERS THE LEAVES—it's the first hard frost. We've had all the clues: golden light falling through the thinning trees patterning the grass, the whiff of wood smoke hanging in cold air, and a certain vibrancy to every view and vista. But a hard frost is the delineator. When we meet at Canal House, we both start talking at the same time "What a day! Fall is really here. Let's take a walk before work." And up the towpath we go, Christopher's little dog, Henry, padding along at our side. We talk as we walk and quickly the conversation turns to food. We think of all the things we'd like to eat now that the cold weather is here. "Let's make sausages...remember that delicious broiled lobster with cream we used to make...gnocchi, definitely gnocchi...and we need to ask Frank Stitt about those grower Champagnes." So we make a list and a plan.

One day we drive into New York to see what's cooking. We're buzzing with excitement and expectation as we drive first through pretty country roads, then onto two-lane highways, and finally we are navigating the four lanes of freeway as we near the city. We chat all the way in about where we are going to go, what we want to buy, then how we plan to cook everything. We are hungry for the elegance of truffles, foie gras, and caviar, and turned on by the idea of making our own fresh sausages, rustic terrines, and roast goose. We're having a good time.

We hit a few stores, and then we head for Russ & Daughters, the venerable appetizing emporium on New York City's Lower East Side, offering the finest smoked fish, pickled and preserved herring, fish roe, and more. Niki Russ Federman and Josh Russ Tupper, fourth-generation Russes, are behind the counter when we walk in and as always, the place is bustling. It's been a year and it's great to see them. They come out from behind the counter to give us a warm hello. We talk about all their wonderful fish and Niki tells us stories while she gives us little tastes. We buy Danish doubled-smoked salmon, chubs with skin that look like burnished gold, salty belly lox, and seven kinds of pickled herring, and we choose jewel-like orange trout roe over osetra caviar—our pockets are only so deep. Everything they sell is so beautifully chosen and prepared.

We load our treasures into coolers in the car. Then we walk across the street to Prune, the restaurant that Melissa's sister Gabrielle owns, and order juicy burgers and flutes of beautiful bubbly Guy Larmandier Rosé, one of those grower Champagnes that we love. On our way out of town we swing by Myers of Keswick for traditional British pork pies and bangers to take home to our families.

It feels so good to cook for ourselves, our families, and our friends at Canal House. We choose small splurges with big returns. We are ready, our larder and fridge are full, and there are a couple bottles of Champagne chilling out on our little balcony. We have everything we need for this season's recipe repertoire. When the kitchen is up and running it's amazing what you can make. Good food begets more good food. And then there is the beautiful bonus of leftovers—a breakfast of jellied juices from last night's roast chicken spread on toast, or a thick slice of pâté on a warm buttered English muffin, or a lunch of minced chicken and mushrooms wrapped up in a delicate crêpe.

Sometimes life arrives at our door unexpectedly. One evening while we were working late, there was a shy knock at the door. Elizabeth and Tom, in their Saturday night finery, stepped into the studio beaming. Walking by after dinner, they'd seen our lights glowing into the dark and climbed the stairs to share some good news. He'd just proposed. She'd accepted. The room turned into a dream—they stood there floating in love. We were transported too, the first to know. Thrilled to share the happy moment, we pulled out a chilled bottle of Champagne, popped the cork, and toasted to their happiness and to a good life to come.

Soon after, Gabrielle arrived from the city with Melissa's two young nephews, Marco and Leone, for a few days in the country. Her visit coincided, unfortunately, with our deadline, a DO NOT DISTURB sign hung on the door. But the boys wanted/needed to say hi to their aunt for just a minute. They met Henry the dog. That minute turned into ten as boys and dog raced around the studio chasing each other. Then off they went on a walk, and returned with Henry wet and covered in mud. Everything stopped. Time for a bath in the sink. The boys helped scrub him up with lots of soapy bubbles. They pulled out the burrs from his long feathery coat. We baked a tray of sugar cookies and gave in to the moment. The ten-minute hello turned into a two-hour adventure for the boys, the dog, and for us. We made our deadline anyway.

The good life surrounds us. We find it in our everyday rituals. But often it comes through the unexpected, too, and we gratefully embrace it.

Christopher & Melissa

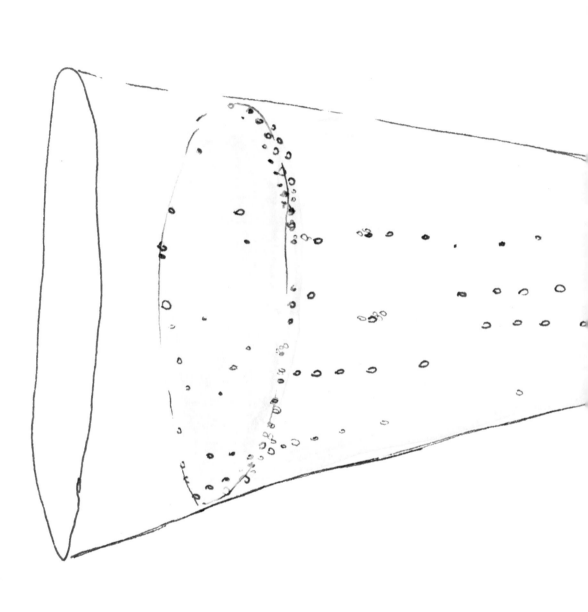

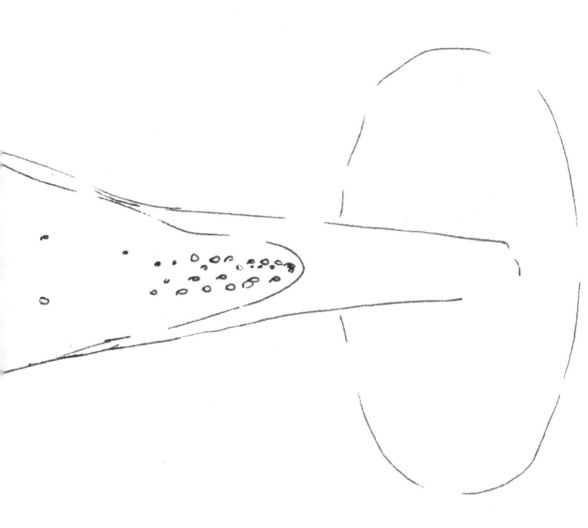

It's always five o'clock somewhere

and never a bad time to pour a glass of something sparkly...

CHRISTMAS EVE
by
GABRIELLE HAMILTON

HE BOYS, MARCO AND LEONE, are the blood and the beat of my four-chambered heart, but there is nothing greater than packing them off to their dad's house on Christmas Eve day, leaving me alone in my apartment for a solid 24. Goodbye little gentlemen, goodbye "Eeewww, mamma! There's something green in my pasta!"; goodbye shrieking, tearful squabble over tubby toy; goodbye bogus games of chess in which your rook takes all of my pawns in one move. See you in the morning, pumpkins!

I lock the door, load the dishwasher, blast the stereo, and sing along at the top of my lungs. My apologies to the upstairs neighbor, but I know every damned word of this thing and have since high school choir and she's going to have to live through my singing every single one of them at top pitch, for—after all—*unto us a son is given.* The crooked must be made straight and the rough places made plain. And to that end, the smell of lemon Cascade wafts out of the dishwasher as the glasses turn crystal clear. *I know that my Redeemer liveth.*

This is not to say that I spend the day relaxing, in the traditional sense. There are some people who just throw the shit in the closet, neaten the bedcovers, and light a cranberry-scented candle, but I am not one of them. With only a few hours until sundown, when my Christmas Eve guests will arrive, it becomes somehow imperative to me—and immensely soothing—to finally artfully hang my collection of antique knife steels, to sort out the Salvation Army clothes from the ones that still have life, to Mop & Glo every inch of the linoleum floor, to crawl out onto the fire escape and clean the outsides of the windows too, to sand down the stains on my butcher block kitchen counter with #57 grade sandpaper, and to arrange the books on the shelves. Not alphabetically. *Please*. That would be so anal-retentive and rigid. But still, you can't let John Berger just lie there next to T. C. Boyle as if they were equals.

I know some of you understand.

A full day alone is magnificent for me. Normally, I spend all 24 in the constant company of others. Having a family and running a busy restaurant pose special challenges to the solitude-loving Scorpio! There are always always people. Even in the quiet early morning prep hours at the restaurant, when I am staring sleepy and vacant at the espresso machine as it drizzles the brown gold into my cup, getting ready for my monster day, even then when the delivery brutes with their weight-lifter belts and pneumatic hand-trucks have not yet come clanking heavily down the hatch stairs and the jug of pine cleaner has not yet been tipped into the porter's mop bucket, there is still Manolo rhythmically sweeping upstairs. And then arrives the daytime sous-chef. And then the phone gal and, soon after, the GM and then we are welcoming lunch guests and wine reps and fire inspectors and then the evening crew shows up, followed by a hundred dinner guests. Even the walk home from work—which is less than half a block and is the daily solitude I can count on—even that is shared with East Village fashionistas teetering down the sidewalk in impossible shoes and too often puking between parked cars.

Home in bed with the boys (because that's our life at the moment until I can afford the space we really need and want) I merely doze throughout the night as some small but remarkably leaden foot or hand smashes me inadvertently in the eye or jaw. To spend the entire day alone—my restaurant shuttered for the holiday (nothing can possibly go wrong at work because there is no work!), kids safely stowed at their dad's while I howl all four parts of Handel's *Messiah* around my apartment—is, for me, the tip of the top of the freshest mountain.

By dark, I am sprinting to be ready for the guests. The apartment is now perfection—the paperwhites have popped and are reeking their narcissus deliciousness in the living room, there are freshly ironed sheets clean and taut on the bed with a duvet and six pillows puffed up like a thick layer of sweet white meringue where guests will throw their coats. On the now spotless old stove, my 10-quart scuffed Le Creuset simmers with a brothy soup thick with nicely cut vegetables. And I have been alone long enough; I'm ready for friends, conversation, laughing my brains out.

I throw myself through a two-minute shower, shave my legs and pits and—why not?—it's not bikini season but... *there*, too. As long as we're getting down to such details as where Berger should rest on the bookshelf we might as well take the same care with our own body. *Rejoice! Rejoice! Re-jo-o-o-o-oice greatly!* With three minutes to go, I dig the accumulated crap out from under my fingernails with a wooden skewer and give them one quick-drying coat of Ballet Slipper. It's Christmas Eve, for Christ's sake.

By the time the intercom buzzes, I am assembling the greatest grilled cheese sandwiches of all time and the fridge is filled with seriously good Champagne, so packed that the bottles that can't stand up on the top shelf lie on their sides like stockpiled ammo down below. This is not the day I want to be drinking any of that chardonnay-sweet or over-yeasted bread-dough shit. I want tight effervescence, chalk on my tongue and the roof of my mouth, sugar turned to cold glass. *WONDERFUL! COUNSELOR! ALMIGHTY GOD!*

I grate the sharp cheddar and slice the blue cheese, sliver fresh mango, and thinly slice a few jalapeños. On the counter is a jar of Hellman's mayonnaise. There may still be a few people who don't know about Hellman's as the perfect and only cooking fat for a grilled cheese sandwich, so here it is: Don't use butter. Don't use oil. Instead, smear a thin film of Hellman's mayonnaise on the outsides of the sandwich and set it in a nonstick pan over low-ish heat. If some of the cheddar melts into the pan, let it set there until it makes that nutty, crunchy lace, which is one of the treats of life.

I like the blue cheese grilled on pumpernickel with a few strips of bacon. But the absolute best is just plain grated cheddar with a little mustard and mayo stirred in to season it. For a second course, I like the cheddar with mango and a few spikes of jalapeño.

The buzzer buzzes and my friends start piling hungrily into my apartment. I fill the crystal flutes to the top, one for everybody, and we clink and cheers. For me, the flute itself hits an especially sweet spot. Almost everything I drink at work I drink out of a plastic quart take-out container which may or may not have had harissa vinaigrette, Bloody Mary mix, or blanched and peeled calf's brains in it the day before. No matter how sanitizing the run through the dish machine is, most of the time my ginger ale tastes weird.

Heidi, my best friend, for whom Christmas Eve with grilled cheese and Champagne is as fixed a ritual as it is for me, at last arrives. For upwards of 15 years, she's brought the shenanigans. The human Christmas tree she and her girlfriend, Diana, the acrobat and aerialist, once made in my living room by one standing on the other's shoulders and holding a star overhead, dressed in green costumes. The lopsided Christmas wreath made of cardboard and tufted tissue paper, whose imperfections and crazy pipe cleaners would make Martha Stewart bust out in a nervous sweat. Soon enough, here she is, changing the lyrics from "He" to "Cheese" and I promise you, you have never laughed so hard as when she empties her lungs, in falsetto, with, *"And Cheese shall pur-i-fy-ihy-ihy-ihy-ihy-ihy-ihy-ihy-ihy-ihy-ihy-ihy. And Cheese shall pu-u-rify."*

I'm in a clean and pretty dress that would matter if I spilled something on it, I've got a real glass filled with very real Champagne, I've managed a spritz of Annick Goutal's Eau d'Hadrien down the old cleavage and Heidi is making me laugh my head off. I'm fully in the Good Life.

After they have all gone, I load the dishwasher anew, squirt the lemon gel into the little compartment, change from my dress into sweats and clogs, and take a cab up to their dad's to sneak in. The boys are deep asleep; I can see their faces, illuminated by the yellow tree lights. The four chambers of my heart flood to see them again.

Gabrielle Hamilton, beloved sister of Melissa, is the chef and owner of Prune, which she opened in New York City's East Village in October 1999. Her forthcoming book, Blood, Bones, and Butter, will be published by Random House in March 2011.

GROWER CHAMPAGNES

I first fell in love with "grower" Champagnes several years ago when Kevin Pike, who distributes wine for the well-known importer Terry Theise, invited me to a portfolio tasting of these wines, and a chance to meet their producers, in New York at Tribeca Grill. We had poured Champagne for years at our restaurant and had been very happy with a major marquee name, Laurent-Perrier, whose consistent quality and style we appreciated. But through these small producers—who bottle just a few thousand cases instead of several million, working the distinctive soils of Champagne to grow all of their own fruit and make them into sparkling wines of immense personality and character—we discovered a whole new world of sparkling finesse. Sometimes called "farmer fizz," the wines come from estates that have been producing Champagne for centuries. But now the younger generation of wine makers have embraced an artisanal approach, and they are making a big impact.

Through Kevin I got to know Terry. At a time when most importers were focusing on one or two big Champagne houses, Terry had found all these different, vivid personalities, and it opened my eyes. It was a bit like discovering the uniqueness of *Grand cru* vineyards, whether they are in the Mosel, Alsace, or Burgundy. Now don't get me wrong, I will never turn down a glass of Krug, but these guys from the small farms of Pierre Peters, Margaine, Gaston Chiquet, and Pehu Simonet provide artisanlike quality at a powerful value.

At almost all restaurants with great wine programs, you will now find an array of these producers, whose names you probably will not recognize. Simply let the sommelier know that you are interested in trying a grower Champagne and soon you'll be introduced to this relatively new category of fine wines. They are more affordable than bottles from the big houses, so pass over the Moët et Chandon and the Taittinger and look for these less familiar bottles—and seek them out at your local wine shop, too. *A votre santé.*

Frank Stitt is the chef and owner of Highlands Bar and Grill, Bottega, Café Bottega, and Chez Fonfon, all in Birmingham, Alabama, and all pouring grower Champagnes.

RM (Récoltant-Manipulant) Meaning roughly "grower-winemaker", who both sells grapes/juice/wine to the big houses and produces their own Champagne using at least 95 percent of their own fruit to make their wine.

SR (Société de Récoltants) Two or more growers, who are often related, share premises to make their Champagne, sometimes under more than one brand label.

NM (Négociant-Manipulant) Indicates that the producer purchased more than 5 percent of their grapes; the wine is not a grower Champagne.

Rosé

Choosing a Rosé versus a more traditional bottle is up to the drinker, but the two are equals when it comes to serious bubbly. Rosé Champagnes gain a hint of color because the juice was left to sit with the dark grape skins for a short stint, or because a small amount of red wine was added to the blend. They often contain more Pinot Noir and Pinot Menuier than Chardonnay, so they typically have a fuller, fruitier style, though, of course, there are exceptions to every rule.

Blanc de Blancs or Blanc de Noirs

By way of introduction to these two terms, it's helpful to know that there are three important grapes in Champagne production and three main regions where grower-winemakers are planting right now. Most Champagne is a blending of these three grapes.

White Chardonnay grapes make up 96 percent of the plantings in the Côte des Blanc region, and some Champagne produced here is 100 percent Chardonnay, in which case it is labeled *Blanc de Blancs*. Chardonnay contributes crisp acidity to a blend and can also provide the yeasty, nutty, or biscuitlike flavors that sometimes appear.

Pinot Noir is the leading grape in the Montagne de Reims region, and it adds softness to the texture of Champagne while also serving as the backbone in many blends. A blend heavy with Pinot Noir may feature more red-berry tones like strawberry, cassis, and raspberry.

The dark purple, almost black Pinot Meunier grape is known for adding richness and body and is planted heavily in the Vallée de la Marne. It provides fleshiness, structure, and lushness. A blend featuring only the two dark-skinned grapes—Pinot Noir and Pinot Meunier without any Chardonnay—is called a *Blanc de Noirs*.

NV (Non-Vintage) and Vintage

Most Champagne is non-vintage, NV on the label, meaning that it was made from a few different vintages blended together. A vintage Champagne will have a date on the label, which indicates that 100 percent of the grapes used to make the wine were harvested in that year. A maker may choose to produce a vintage Champagne if they've had a particularly impressive harvest year. A vintage Champagne must be aged for at least three years before release, while a NV bottling is only required to age for one year.

Cru

Cru is the French word for "growth place." In the Champagne region, the terms Premier Cru (sometimes "1st Cru" on labels for the American market) and Grand Cru refer to the villages where the grapes were grown, rather than vineyards or estates, and were a way of denoting wines of superior quality ("Grand" being the top level). These days the system is less valuable, since the quality of crop varies from grower to grower rather than village to village.

Extra Brut, Brut, and Extra Sec

The dryness of a wine indicates how acidic (versus sweet) it is. Extra Brut is the driest, then Brut—the most common—followed by Extra Sec, which is a bit sweeter than brut.

Other Terms: Sélection Réserve, Grande Réserve, Spécial Réserve, Cuvée

All of these terms mean that the winemaker decided that the bottling was in some way superior to his regular production. The terms are not regulated, but can help you choose between two bottles from the same producer. You might splurge for the Grande Réserve, which will be more expensive than the same maker's entry-level bottling, for instance. The word cuvée, which means "vat," could signal any number of things. A cuvée name for a bottling (Cuvée Saint Denis, for example) might mean that the grapes in the bottling are from a specific vineyard plot that the grower has deemed especially expressive of the terroir. However, it could also refer to a special blend.

Village Name

The label will also list the village where the Champagne was made and the address of the estate in very small print.

Who is Selecting and Importing the Champagne?

And finally (some would say most important), check out the label on the back of the bottle. It will tell you who selected and/or imported the Champagne. Most of the recommended bottles below are the selection of Kermit Lynch Wine Merchant, Rosenthal Wine Merchant, Selection Becky Wasserman, and Terry Theise Estate Selections. All have exquisite taste, search high and low to find the finest wines, and stake their reputation on the producers they choose to represent.

OUR FAVORITE FARMER FIZZES

A. Margaine "Special Club" Blanc de Blancs, Brut, 2002—100 percent Chardonnay. Just down the road from Veuve Clicquot, in the village of Villers-Marmery, is Arnaud Margaine. Making Champagnes with striking aromas, Margaine made a surprising move by planting 90 percent of his parcels with Chardonnay—in Pinot Noir country. The "Special Club" is his top cuvée from 2002 and has warm gingerbread notes. The Special Club is a collective of 26 top RM producers. The club members taste each other's top cuvées and decide which are worthy of the "Special Club" designation and the vintage bottle shape. Gimonnet, Bara, Hébrart, and Lassalle are also members of the club.

Diebolt-Vallois à Cramant, Brut, NV—40 percent Chardonnay, 35 percent Pinot Noir, 35 percent Pinot Meunier. This family estate produces refreshing, bracing Champagne in the village of Cramant, in the Côte des Blancs region. The acidity is like crisp green apple, but the body is full, like a beautiful Chablis. They are registered as NM, but they do grow most of their own fruit.

Godmé Père & Fils Blanc de Noirs, Brut, NV—100 percent Pinot Noir. From the village of Verzenay, where red grapes outnumber white, comes this smoky Blanc de Noirs. It has flavors of toasted nuts, vanilla, burnt orange, brown butter, and chewy fruit skin, and is best served with food rather than as an aperitif.

Guy Larmandier Rosé, Brut, NV—82 percent Chardonnay, 12 percent Pinot Noir. The pretty pink color will make you think of sweet fruit, but this rosé is exceptionally dry, with almost no dosage (added sugar). It's been called the Billecart-Salmon of the grower Champagnes, and is beautiful and fresh. The brand began as Larmandier Père & Fils, and the family tree includes Pierre Gimonnet and Larmandier-Bernier.

J. Lassalle, Réserve Cachet d'Or, Brut, NV—60 percent Pinot Meunier, 25 percent Chardonnay, 15 percent Pinot Noir. Importer Kermit Lynch says this is what the

Domaine Tempier family likes to drink on special occasions. It has liveliness, soft acidity, and elegance. Lassalle's Champagnes from Chigny-les-Roses are rich and perfumed.

Marc Hébrart "Sélection", Brut, NV—65 percent Pinot Noir, 35 percent Chardonnay. Hébrart grows mostly Pinot Noir in the esteemed village of Mareuil-sur-Aÿ, where the grape makes impressive Champagnes that are firm and finessed, yet chalky. Hébrart is married to Isabelle Diebolt of Diebolt-Vallois and he sources some Chardonnay from her family estate. The "Sélection" has flavors of mandarin, saffron, and persimmon.

Paul Bara Grand Rosé, Brut, NV—75 percent Pinot Noir, 12.5 percent Chardonnay, 12.5 percent Bouzy Rouge. Though Pinot Meunier is planted most often in the Marne, the renown village of Bouzy is almost all Pinot Noir plantings. Made from 30-year-old vines, this pink-orange Rosé has a complex mix of spice, raspberry tartness, citrus fruit, and good minerality.

Pehu-Simonet "Sélection" Brut, NV—70 percent Pinot Noir, 30 percent Chardonnay. This delicious wine, from a tiny producer in Verzenay, has a bright blue label and is often described as rich, malty, with lush apple. Frank Stitt serves it by the glass at Highlands Bar and Grill, Bottega, and Café Bottega.

Pierre Gimonnet et Fils "Cuvée Gastronome", Brut, 2004 —100 percent Chardonnay. Didier Gimonnet named this Champagne Gastronome because its smaller, more delicate, less intrusive bubbles make it the perfect Champagne to drink with food.

René Geoffroy "Cuvée Expression", Brut, NV—50 percent Pinot Meunier, 40 percent Pinot Noir, 10 percent Chardonnay. True enthusiasm surrounds Jean-Baptiste Geoffroy. Kevin Pike at Terry Theise Estate Selections calls him "the most fanatical wine-freak I know in Champagne." He recently built a brand-new production in Aÿ and makes vibrant, fruity cuvées with warm flavors, mostly from red grapes.

Varnier-Fannière "Cuvée Saint Denis", Brut, NV—100 percent Chardonnay. This Blanc de Blancs from 70-year-old vines is one of the best values available. It's the finest bottling of this tiny estate in the village of Avize, with mouthwatering fruit, toasted hazelnut, and the pencil-lead graphite quality that distinguishes this village.

Veuve Fourny et Fils Grande Réserve, Brut, NV—80 percent Chardonnay, 20 percent Pinot Noir. The Fourny family has been making Champagne for four generations in the village of Vertus. This cuvée is made with fruit from 35-year-old vines and has pretty citrus hints of Meyer lemon. It's classified as an NM on the label, but the Fournys only buy grapes from family and friends who follow the RM philosophy.

wørking up an appetite

AN APPETIZING SMØRREBRØD

One of the rituals we look forward to as the cold weather holidays approach is stocking up on and indulging in all varieties of delicious smoked and cured fish and a few kinds of fish roe—they pair perfectly with a glass of cold Champagne. At the "appetizing" shops in New York City ("appetizing" being the term for stores that sell fish and dairy that traditionally start off a meal), everything comes beautifully prepared and ready to eat: silky, buttery smoked salmons, pickled herring filets, affordable jewel-like orange trout and salmon eggs, and expensive grey-black caviars, too. We rely on one of the oldest appetizing shops in the country, Russ & Daughters, established in 1914—a New York City institution on the Lower East Side.

And every year we assemble our version of the famed *smørrebrød* (Danish for "buttered bread")—that glorious array of open-faced sand-wiches. We make them with all the fish from our "appetizing" spree. We prepare a few simple spreads and condiments that work with most every-thing so it's easy to mix and match. Here are the things we like to have on hand for building these beautiful sandwiches.

⤛ BREAD ⤜

We use thin slices of good, dense, black rye or pumpernickel.

⤛ SPREADS ⤜

To keep the bread moist and keep the toppings from making it soggy, we use a few different spreads.

Butter—Our standard. We use a delicious salted butter, like the Irish butter from Kerrygold, kept at room temperature so it's easy to spread.

Creamed cheese—We like to use goat cream cheese when we can find it.

HORSERADISH BUTTER

Mix together 4 tablespoons softened butter with 1–2 tablespoons drained prepared horseradish in a small bowl until smooth. This butter will keep, covered, in the refrigerator for up to 1 week. —— *makes about ¼ cup*

Overleaf: The Canal House smørrebrød spread

We like a selection of pickled, smoked, cured, and tinned fish, and use some or all of the following, depending on how ambitious we are feeling.

Belly lox—This is the mid-section of a juicy salmon, cured in a special salt brine. We love its tingly saltiness.

Chub—These smoky North American lake fish are tender and moist.

Smoked sablefish—An appetizing classic, this buttery smoked fish, also known as black cod or simply sable, is line-caught in the waters of the North Pacific.

Pickled, smoked, salted, and matjes herring—We love them all, from the classic briny pickled herring, to the smoky French herring, to the salted schmaltz, and the clovy matjes.

Smoked or cured salmon—With so many available, we've found that the best way to choose is simply to taste your way through, though we avoid those with an artificial-looking pink or orange hue, and ultimately settle on smoked salmon with a good pedigree, and with silky buttery texture well balanced in the salt and smoke world.

Smoked sturgeon—This freshwater white-fleshed fish, whose roe is turned into the priciest kind of caviar, has a distinctly earthy, sweet flavor.

Fish roe—Big orange salmon eggs or beautiful smaller (also orange) trout eggs add a pop-in-your-mouth texture and saltiness; plus they have a jewel-like beauty. Look for malossol quality. We crown sandwiches with a spoonful.

Canned sardines—We like them packed in olive oil. The plump Spanish sardines from Matiz Gallego (three to a can) are excellent.

Canned smoked eel—These delicate little filets have a subtle smoky flavor. We prefer the ones packed in olive oil to those in cottonseed oil.

Canned codfish liver—Not at all like the infamous daily dose, these are rich yet delicate in flavor, and incredibly tender.

GARNISHES

Not just superfluous flourishes to decorate each sandwich, these add an extra hit of flavor.

Radishes—Sliced into thin little matchsticks, they add a pretty, peppery bite.

Preserved lemons—We dice the rind and use it for its vibrant yellow color and bright salty flavor.

Fresh dill—Its delicate, fresh flavor is a classic with preserved fish and its feathery leaves are perfect for garnishing.

Fresh chives—Either finely sliced or cut into longer lengths, they add a hit of green and mild onion flavor.

Hard-boiled eggs—We slice them into rounds and lay them under or over fish or roe.

Boiled potatoes—We like their earthiness underneath the flavors of these cured fish, and we slice them into thin rounds.

QUICK PICKLES

Simple, bright, and colorful pickles like these are a traditional foil for the rich flavors and supple textures of smoked and cured fish. We prepare ours using Japanese rice wine vinegar, because we like the way its perfect balance of sweetness and acidity complement the fish. When making the cucumber or red onion pickles, make only what you need for the meal; the extra slices will go limp after too long a soak.

PICKLED CUCUMBERS

Use the little narrow Japanese or "gourmet" cucumbers for these if you can find them, otherwise an English, seedless one will do. Put thin slices of cucumber in a bowl. Cover with Japanese rice wine vinegar and let them soak for at least 15 minutes and up to 1 hour.

PICKLED RED ONIONS

Soak thin slices of red onion in a bowl of rice wine vinegar for at least 15 minutes and up to 1 hour.

PICKLED CARROTS

Blanch thick round slices of peeled carrot in boiling water; drain and put into a bowl. Cover the carrots with rice wine vinegar, add a few cloves, black peppercorns, and/or a bay leaf, and cool to room temperature. Cover and refrigerate for at least 1 day and up to 2 weeks.

PICKLED BEETS

Wrap beets in foil and roast them in a preheated 400° oven until tender, about 1 hour. Peel and thickly slice the beets and put into a bowl. Cover with rice wine vinegar, add a few cloves, black peppercorns, and/or a bay leaf, and cool to room temperature. Cover and refrigerate for at least 1 day and up to 2 weeks.

MUSTARD-DILL SAUCE

The classic Swedish accompaniment to gravlax and delicious with these sandwiches, too. Put ¼ cup Dijon mustard, 2 tablespoons chopped fresh dill, 2 tablespoons sugar, and ½ teaspoon white wine vinegar into a small bowl and whisk in ¼ cup vegetable oil until smooth.——*makes ½ cup*

Holland herring

FRIED OYSTERS
makes 2 dozen

We usually pry open these sometimes recalcitrant bivalves ourselves for when we are slurping them down ice cold on the half shell, brimming with their briny juice. But when we're frying them, we order the oysters freshly shucked from our fishmonger, requesting smaller varieties because we prefer a higher ratio of crispy crunch to soft, briny meat.

24 shucked oysters, drained
1 cup flour
1–2 eggs, lightly beaten

1–2 cups panko
Vegetable oil
Salt

Dredge each oyster in flour, then in egg, then in panko, and set aside. Add enough oil to a heavy medium pot to reach a depth of about 2 inches. Heat the oil over medium heat until hot but not smoking, ideally to a temperature of 350° (use a candy thermometer to check the temperature or dip a wooden chopstick into the hot oil so that the tip touches the bottom of the pot; if lots of bubbles form right away around the tip, the oil should be ready for frying).

Deep-fry the oysters, a few at a time, until golden brown all over, about 1 minute. Using a slotted fish spatula or spoon, transfer the oysters to a wire rack set over paper towels to drain. Season with salt and serve piping hot.

ESCARGOTS SANS THEIR SHELLS

We use large, delicious wild Burgundy snails from France, packed 2 dozen to a 7-ounce can, and we don't bother stuffing them into shells. Drain the snails, then put them into a small pot with ½ cup Riesling and ½ cup rich veal or chicken stock. Bring to a boil over medium heat and cook for 2 minutes. Remove the pot from the heat and let the snails cool in the broth. Prepare the snail butter by mixing together ½ cup finely chopped parsley leaves, 1 minced shallot, 1–3 minced garlic cloves, pinch of ground anise, and grated zest from half an orange into 12 tablespoons (1½ sticks) softened salted butter. Divide the snails between 4 snail plates or onto slices of baguette in 4 ovenproof dishes. Slather a good dollop of snail butter on each snail and heat in a 300° oven for about 10 minutes. Serve with slices of crusty bread. —— *serves 4*

Big Livers

GOOSE LIVER & PORK TERRINE
serves 10–12

For this classic French country terrine we love Late Harvest Fatty Goose Livers, available through Schiltz Goose Farms, for their pale color and delicate silky texture. Refrigerate the terrine for a couple of days before serving to allow its flavor to develop. Serve, on a slice of toasted country bread, with cornichons.

2 tablespoons goose fat or butter
1 large yellow onion, finely chopped
2 cloves garlic, minced
2 bay leaves
1 teaspoon ground allspice
1 teaspoon ground mace
Salt and pepper
1 pound fatty goose livers,
  or chicken livers

2 pounds ground pork shoulder
½ pound fatback, cut in tiny cubes
3 tablespoons chopped fresh
  thyme leaves
3 tablespoons chopped fresh
  parsley leaves
¼ cup Calvados or Cognac
¼ cup port
1 egg, lightly beaten

Melt the goose fat in a skillet over medium heat. Add the onions, garlic, bay leaves, allspice, and mace, and season with salt and pepper. Cook, stirring from time to time, until the onions are soft but not browned, about 20 minutes. Transfer from the skillet into a large bowl and set side to cool. Remove the bay leaves, you'll use them later.

Preheat the oven to 325°. Set aside 3 goose livers, then chop the remaining livers. When the onions have cooled, add the chopped livers, pork shoulder, fatback, thyme, parsley, Calvados, port, and egg, and season generously with salt and pepper. (You can fry a little of the mixture then taste to be sure it is seasoned correctly; adjust if you need to.) Use your hands to mix everything together. Fill a 6-cup terrine with half of the pâté mixture, then place the reserved goose livers down the middle of the terrine. Add the remaining pâté mixture and shape the surface into a slight dome. Place the bay leaves on top. Set the terrine in a roasting pan then add enough hot water to come three-quarters of the way up the side of the terrine. Cover with a lid or foil.

Put in the oven and cook for 1½ hours. Uncover for the last 15 minutes. Remove from oven, allow to cool, then refrigerate for 2 days before serving.

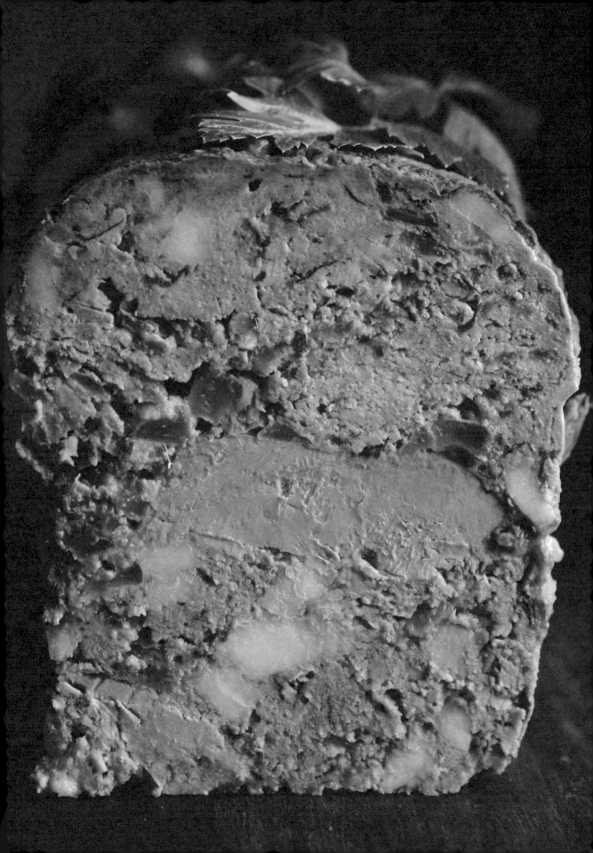

GOOSE LIVER PÂTÉ WITH TRUFFLES
makes 2½ cups

We like to dress up chicken liver pâté for the holidays using plump goose livers from Schiltz Goose Farms, fine Cognac, and a fresh black winter truffle. It's boozy, rich, and elegant served on toast points—the perfect holiday canapé.

If you can't find goose livers, use chicken. If adding a fresh black truffle is out of the question, simply omit it. Substituting canned ones isn't worth it. But do use a full-fat European-style butter and you won't go wrong.

1 pound (4 sticks) butter, softened
1 pound goose livers, cut into thirds
1 small onion, finely chopped
½ cup Cognac

Salt and pepper
1 fresh black winter truffle,
  thinly sliced

Melt 4 tablespoons of the butter in a large skillet over medium-high heat. Add the livers and sauté them on each side until nicely browned on the outside and just pink in the center, 4–5 minutes. Turn off the heat. Stir in the onions and ¼ cup of Cognac. Season well with salt and pepper.

Transfer everything in the skillet to the bowl of a food processor and pulse to a coarse paste. Press pâté mixture through a fine sieve into a large clean bowl. Let cool to room temperature. Use a wooden spoon to beat in remaining 3½ sticks of butter, a few knobs at a time, beating well after each addition. Save the prettiest truffle slice for garnish and finely chop the rest. Beat in chopped truffles and the remaining ¼ cup of Cognac. Adjust seasonings.

Spoon the pâté into a 3-cup terrine or dish and lay the slice of truffle on top. Tightly cover the dish in plastic wrap without letting it touch the pâté and refrigerate until firm, about 8 hours. The pâté will keep for up to 1 week.

TOAST POINTS ❋ Sandwiching (no pun intended) the bread between baking sheets keeps their edges from curling as they bake. Cut the crust off very thin sliced white bread. Halve the slices diagonally. Brush both sides with melted butter. Lay the slices out on a cookie sheet and set another cookie sheet directly on top. Bake in a preheated 400° oven until golden brown on the bottom, 5–10 minutes. Turn the toasts over, cover, and bake until the other side is golden, a few minutes more.

FOIE GRAS AU TORCHON
serves about 12

Don't be afraid to pull apart the foie gras to remove the veins. It will all come back together when you wrap it up in the cheesecloth. By the time the foie has spent a couple of days nestled in its bed of salt, it will be cured and ready to eat.

2 pounds fresh Grade A foie gras
  (fattened duck liver)
1 teaspoon Maldon salt
½ teaspoon ground white pepper
⅛ teaspoon ground cloves

⅛ teaspoon ground cinnamon
⅛ teaspoon ground nutmeg
⅛ teaspoon ground ginger
2 tablespoons Cognac
Kosher salt

Allow the foie gras to come to room temperature, it will be easier to work with when you are cleaning it. Pull the lobes apart and using your fingers or a knife tip, follow the veins and sinews through the meat, gently pulling and lifting them out. Mix the salt, pepper, cloves, cinnamon, nutmeg, and ginger together in a small bowl. Sprinkle the spices then the Cognac all over the cleaned foie gras.

Lay out a 2-foot square of cheesecloth. Place the foie on the cheesecloth, forming it into a block shape. Tightly roll up the cheesecloth, shaping the foie gras into a fat sausage shape. Twist the ends to tighten the cheesecloth and tie with kitchen string.

Pour kosher salt into a deep ceramic dish to a depth of about 1½ inches. Place the foie gras in center, then cover completely with more salt. Place a flat pan on top and weight it with heavy cans. Refrigerate for 2 days.

Lift from the salt and unwrap. Serve thick slices on hot toast with preserved quince or apple. Or use a swivel-type vegetable peeler to shave pieces of foie gras over a crisp lettuce salad. Rewrap in plastic to store for up to 2 days.

BRIOCHE TOASTS

The tender crumb and sweetness of brioche makes wonderful toasts for this silky foie gras. Brush both sides of sliced brioche with melted butter. Lay the slices out on a cookie sheet and set another cookie sheet directly on top. Bake in a preheated 400° oven until golden brown on the bottom, about 10 minutes. Turn the toasts over, cover, and bake until the other side is golden, a few minutes more.

SEARED FOIE GRAS WITH GREEN GRAPES
serves 4–8

For this luxurious classic from the south-west of France, use the larger of the two lobes from a fresh whole foie gras in order to slice beautiful thick pieces. Save the smaller lobe to make Foie Gras au Tourchon (page 35), if you like. (Can you ever have too much of a good thing?) Tightly wrapped in plastic, it will keep for a few days in the fridge. (We do not recommend freezing non–vacuum-packed foie gras.) Or, to make life a little easier, consider buying pre-sliced fresh foie gras.

FOR THE SAUCE

1 cup finest seedless green grapes

1½ cups Muscat, Sauternes, or late-harvest Riesling

1 cup chicken stock

1 tablespoon white wine vinegar

¼ teaspoon freshly grated nutmeg

¼ cup heavy cream

Salt and white pepper

FOR THE FOIE GRAS

1 large lobe fresh Grade A foie gras, sliced to make 4 diagonal pieces, 4–5 ounces each

¼ cup very fine dry plain bread crumbs

Maldon or other sea salt

For the sauce, blanch the grapes in boiling water in a heavy medium saucepan for 1 minute; drain. Peel the grapes and set aside. Put the wine into the pan and bring to a boil over medium-high heat, reducing it to about ¼ cup, about 10 minutes. It will have a syrupy consistency. Add the stock, vinegar, and nutmeg and boil until thickened a bit and reduced almost by half, about 5 minutes. Add the cream and boil until the sauce is just thick enough to coat the back of a spoon, about 2 minutes. Add the peeled grapes and swirl them around in the sauce. Reduce the heat to low. Season with salt and pepper. Keep it warm over very low heat.

For the foie gras, dust each piece with bread crumbs and season with salt. Heat a large nonstick skillet over medium-high heat until hot but not smoking. Add the foie gras, then move the skillet off the heat briefly. Reduce the heat to medium. Return the skillet to the heat and finish searing the foie gras, turning it halfway through, until deep golden brown, 1–1½ minutes per side. Transfer the foie gras with a slotted spatula to warm plates and spoon the sauce and grapes around it. Sprinkle a little salt on top of each serving.

uova huevos oeufs eggs

SCRAMBLED EGGS WITH TRUFFLES
serves 2–4

The experience of eating these buttery soft-scrambled eggs perfumed with the heady, intimate fragrance of truffle is powerful. Choose your company wisely.

Thinly slice 1 fresh black winter truffle, reserving 8 slices for garnish. Chop remaining slices and put them in a medium bowl. Add 6 eggs, 3 tablespoons heavy cream, and some salt (preferably Maldon sea salt) and pepper.

Melt 4 tablespoons butter in a medium skillet over medium-high heat. Lightly beat the eggs and truffles and pour them into the bubbling butter. After a few seconds, pull the set egg into center of the skillet using a spatula. The uncooked egg will rush out to the edges. Wait until more egg begins to set again then pull that into the center, making big soft curds. Continue doing this until all the eggs are softly set, about 2 minutes in total. Serve the eggs garnished with the truffle slices and sprinkled with salt.

PIQUILLO PEPPER EGGS
serves 2

Distinctive little cone-shaped, fire-roasted piquillo peppers, from Spain's Navarra region, give a sweet earthiness to these delicious, delicate eggs.

¼ cup extra-virgin olive oil
1 medium onion, cut lengthwise
  into medium-thick slices
1 clove garlic, thinly sliced
6–8 canned piquillo peppers,
  drained

1 egg
½ cup heavy cream
Salt and pepper
3 slices Manchego or other cheese
  of your choice
Small handful torn parsley leaves

Preheat oven to 375°. Heat the oil in a medium skillet over medium-high heat. Add the onions and garlic and sauté until lightly browned, about 10 minutes.

Arrange the peppers in a small gratin dish and tuck the onions and garlic around them, drizzling in any oil from the skillet. Lightly beat the egg and the cream together and season with salt and pepper. Pour over the peppers. Arrange the cheese on top. Bake until the custard is slightly puffed and golden, about 20 minutes. Season with a little more salt and garnish with parsley.

PIMENTÓN FRIED EGGS

We love the rich, savory flavor of eggs fried in bubbling hot olive oil and the way the oil makes the whites puffy around the yolks and crisp around the edges. Pimentón, the exquisite Spanish paprika, adds a delicious smoky flavor and stains the oil a gorgeous deep brick orange, so beautiful to baste over the eggs. Serve these for breakfast, with a good crusty bread to sop up the flavorful oil, or with stewy chickpeas any time of the day.

Heat 4 tablespoons olive oil in a heavy medium skillet over medium-high heat until quite warm. Add ½ teaspoon pimentón and tip the skillet to swirl it around so it dissolves into the oil. Crack 4 eggs into the skillet and reduce the heat if it gets a little too hot. Fry the eggs, basting them with the olive oil, until the whites are firm and the yolks remain soft. Season with salt. Serve the eggs with the oil spooned on top.—*makes 4*

EGGS WITH CAPER & PARSLEY BUTTER SAUCE
makes about ¼ cup

This piquant sauce is lovely spooned over poached or fried eggs, but is equally delicious served with a filet of flounder, sole, or other delicate white fish.

4 tablespoons butter
2 tablespoons red or white
   wine vinegar
1 tablespoon capers

2–3 tablespoons chopped fresh
   parsley leaves
4 poached or fried eggs

Melt the butter in a small pan over medium heat. When it is foaming, add the vinegar and capers and cook, swirling the pan over the heat from time to time, until the vinegar evaporates, the butter browns slightly, and the sauce thickens a little bit, 1–2 minutes. Remove the pan from the heat and add the parsley. Spoon the sauce over the eggs.

Crêpes

BROILED PIG'S FEET CRÊPES
makes 16

These savory crêpes, with their rich, sticky filling, will put hair on your chinny chin chin. They are gutsy and completely delicious, but you have to love big flavors, like we do, to enjoy them. We began making these in the mid-1980s when tapas were a new concept in this country, thanks in part, to Penelope Casas, from whose seminal book, *Tapas: The Little Dishes of Spain* (Knopf, 1985), this recipe is adapted.

FOR THE CRÊPES
2 pig's feet (1 pound each), split
4 fresh ham hocks (½ pound each)
2 ounces slab bacon
1 carrot, peeled and cut into thirds
2 small yellow onions, halved
5 cups chicken stock
3 cups red wine
1 branch fresh thyme
1 bay leaf
4 peppercorns
4 cloves
Salt
12 tablespoons butter, melted

2 cloves garlic, minced
10 ounces white mushrooms, finely chopped
2 tablespoons chopped fresh parsley
1 tablespoon dry white wine
Pepper
16 crêpes (facing page)

FOR THE ALIOLI
1 large egg yolk
3–4 cloves garlic, minced to a paste
Salt
½ teaspoon fresh lemon juice
1 cup "buttery" olive oil

For the crêpes, put the feet, hocks, bacon, carrots, 1 of the onions, stock, red wine, thyme, bay leaf, peppercorns, cloves, and a pinch of salt in a large heavy pot. Cover and simmer over medium-low heat until the feet and hocks are very tender, about 5 hours. Strain, discarding all but the feet and hocks; reserve the flavorful broth for another use. Pick through the meats, discarding only the bones and any tough cartilage. Mince the meat, skin, soft cartilage, and fat.

Mince the remaining onion. Heat 6 tablespoons of the butter in a large skillet over medium heat. Cook the onions until soft. Add the garlic, mushrooms, and parsley and cook for 3–5 minutes. Stir in the minced meat and cook for 5 minutes. Remove the skillet from the heat. Stir in the white wine and season well with salt and pepper.

Put about ¼ cup of the filling on each crêpe and roll it up around the filling.

For the alioli, whisk together the egg yolk, garlic, pinch of salt, and lemon juice in a medium bowl. Add oil 1 teaspoon at a time, whisking constantly. The sauce will thicken and emulsify. After adding about ¼ cup of the oil, begin slowly drizzling in the remaining oil, whisking constantly, until sauce is thick. Season with salt.

Preheat the broiler. Spread the alioli over the bottom of 1 or 2 baking dishes. Arrange crêpes on top, seam side down. Brush them with the remaining butter. Broil until golden brown, 1–2 minutes. Serve crêpes whole or cut in half.

CRÊPES
makes about 8

Richard Olney writes about crêpes and their versatility with great affection in *Simple French Food* (Penguin, 1983)—eaten sweet (dessert crêpes) and nonsweet (savory crêpes) alike. After years of sweetening his dessert crêpe batter with sugar, as most recipes call for, he realized he preferred them unsweetened—a dessert crêpe is sweet enough, he reasoned, without adding more sweetness to the batter. We've followed his lead and omit sugar from our recipe below, which can be used, conveniently, for making either sweet or savory crêpes. They are delicious eaten straight from the pan spread with soft butter or jam, buttered and sugared, rolled up with a thin slice of ham and finely grated Gruyère, or warmed up one at a time in a bit of melted butter in a skillet over medium heat with any of the dessert crêpe fillings on page 49. Use this batter to make the Broiled Pig's Feet Crêpes on the facing page as well.

Though crêpe batter can be used right away, the crêpes will be more tender if the batter has rested for an hour. This recipe can easily be doubled and the batter will keep in the refrigerator, covered, for up to 2 days.

¼ cup flour	1 tablespoon Cognac, optional
⅛ teaspoon salt	¼ cup milk
3 eggs, lightly beaten	4 tablespoons butter, melted

Combine the flour and salt in a medium bowl. Whisk in the eggs and Cognac. Gradually add the milk, whisking until smooth, then stir in the melted butter.

continued

Strain the batter through a sieve into a small pitcher or a bowl. Let rest for 1–2 hours.

Heat a seasoned crêpe pan or medium nonstick skillet over medium-high heat. Grease pan by rubbing it with a little butter. Stir batter, then pour about 2 tablespoons batter into the pan, tilting and rotating it the minute the batter hits the pan. Quickly swirl batter around so that it coats the bottom of the pan in a very thin, even layer. Pour any excess batter back into the pitcher. When the crêpe surface is set, the edges curl, and the underside is golden, about 1 minute, turn it over with your fingers or a thin spatula. Cook other side until pale golden in spots, about 30 seconds. Turn pan upside down and tip crêpe out onto a plate. (Your first couple of crêpes may not be successful, but keep going until you get the hang of it.) Repeat with remaining batter, making about 8 crêpes in all. Serve crêpes warmed one at a time in a bit of melted butter in a skillet over medium heat with any of the fillings below. Crêpes keep, stacked between sheets of wax paper and wrapped in plastic wrap, in the fridge for up to a week or in the freezer for up to a month.

BUCKWHEAT CRÊPES VARIATION: Follow the recipe above for making crêpes, reducing the all-purpose flour to 1 tablespoon and adding 3 tablespoons buckwheat flour, and reducing the melted butter to 2 tablespoons.

DESSERT CRÊPES

LEMON SUGAR CRÊPES: Combine the finely grated zest of 1 lemon with 1 cup sugar. Put a warm crêpe (page 47) on a plate and spread it with some soft butter. Squeeze some fresh lemon juice over the crêpe and sprinkle with 1–2 tablespoons of the lemon sugar. Repeat with remaining crêpes and lemon sugar. —— *makes 8*

ORANGE SUGAR CRÊPES: Follow the directions for making Lemon Sugar Crêpes, substituting finely grated zest of 1 orange for the lemon zest and a splash of Cointreau for the lemon juice. —— *makes 8*

CHOCOLATE & TOASTED HAZELNUT CRÊPES: Stir ½ cup hot heavy cream into 3 ounces chopped chocolate until smooth. Spread a spoonful of the chocolate sauce over a warm crêpe (page 47). Sprinkle a small handful of chopped, peeled, toasted hazelnuts on top. —— *makes 8*

PEAR & GORGONZOLA CRÊPES: Put 1–2 ounces soft Gorgonzola dolce on a warm crêpe (page 47). Arrange peeled slices of half a perfectly ripe pear on top. —— *makes 1*

BUCKWHEAT BLINI WITH SMOKED SALMON & TROUT ROE
makes about 2 dozen

Little yeasted buckwheat pancakes like these are traditionally served during Maslenitsa, the Russian pre-Lent festivities. At Canal House, we celebrate our holidays each year by serving these blini with the best smoked salmon and gorgeous trout eggs, toasting to the season with a glass of cold Champagne.

FOR THE BLINI
1 cup milk
3 tablespoons butter, diced
1¼ teaspoons active dry yeast
½ cup buckwheat flour
½ cup all-purpose flour
1½ tablespoons sugar
½ teaspoon salt
2 eggs, lightly beaten

TO SERVE
8–12 tablespoons butter, melted
8–12 ounces thinly sliced smoked salmon, each slice cut in half or into thirds
¼ cup sour cream or crème fraîche
4 ounces trout or salmon roe

For the blini, heat milk and butter together in a small saucepan over medium-low heat until butter melts. Remove from heat. If the milk is quite hot, let it cool to between 110° and 115°. Dissolve the yeast in the warm milk.

Whisk together the flours, sugar, and salt in a medium bowl. Add the warm milk, gently whisking until the batter is just combined. Cover bowl with plastic wrap and let the batter rise in a warm spot until it has doubled in size, about 1 hour. Once the batter has risen, you can finish making the blini or transfer the bowl to the refrigerator. The batter will keep for up to 24 hours. Deflate the batter with a whisk, then whisk in the eggs.

Rub a large skillet with a little butter then heat over medium heat. Drop table-spoonfuls of batter into the hot skillet a couple inches apart. Cook until little bubbles form on the surface and begin to pop, 1–2 minutes. Carefully turn blini over and cook other side until golden brown, 1–1½ minutes. Repeat with re-maining batter. Keep blini warm, wrapped in a clean dish towel, in a 200° oven.

To serve, brush the prettier side of each warm blini with some melted butter. Top each blini with a piece of salmon, a bit of sour cream, and a spoonful of roe. Arrange blini on a serving platter and serve right away. They'll go fast.

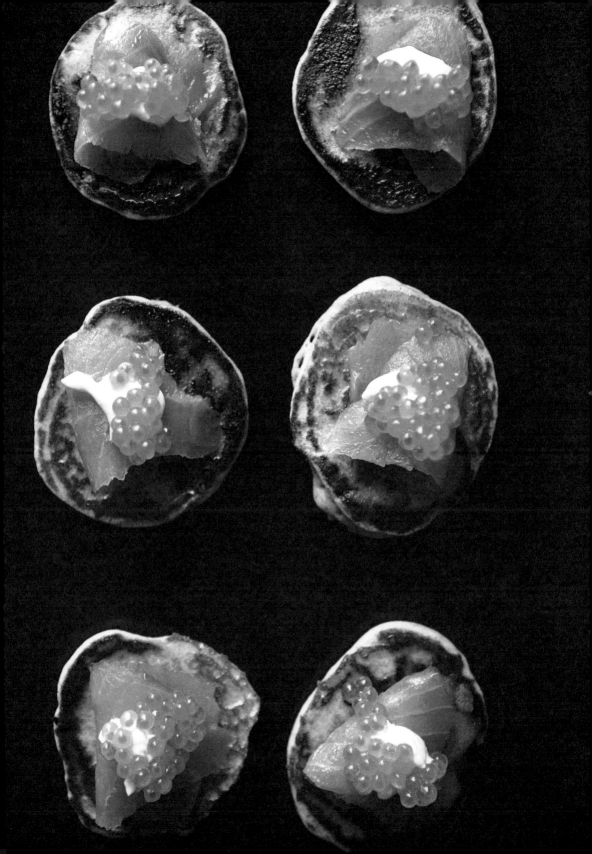

Grandma's

Gnocchi

OUR IMAGINARY GRANDMOTHER'S GNOCCHI
serves 4–6

Since neither of us grew up standing by the apron strings of our very own Italian *nonna* taking in the nuances of making delicate potato dumplings, we had to teach ourselves. Recipes vary. Some insist on starting off with boiled waxy potatoes, others are emphatic about using baked russets. Then there is the issue of the egg. Gnocchi made without egg may be more tender but it can be trickier to work with, dissolving away to nothing in the simmering water if the balance of potato to flour isn't just right. We've landed on this method—using baked russet potatoes and egg—to make these lovely (and tender) little dumplings. We think they're good enough to pass down to the next generation.

2 pounds russet potatoes (2–4 potatoes, depending on their size)
1 large egg, lightly beaten
1 cup all-purpose flour

Salt
6 tablespoons butter, melted
Freshly grated parmigiano-reggiano

Preheat the oven to 400°. Prick the potatoes in several places with a fork. Put the potatoes directly on the oven rack and bake them until soft when pierced with the tip of a sharp knife, about 1 hour.

While the potatoes are still hot, cut one potato at a time in half lengthwise. Scoop out the flesh with a large spoon and push it through a potato ricer (or through a sturdy sieve with the back of a wooden spoon) onto a clean work

surface. Spread out the riced potatoes so the heat and moisture evaporate quickly. Let the potatoes cool completely.

Gather the potatoes into a shallow mound and make a well in the center. Add the eggs to the well. Sift ¾ cup of the flour over the mound. Using a pastry scraper or a metal spatula, work the flour and egg into the potatoes, scraping and folding the mass together until a rough dough forms. Clean the work surface and lightly dust it with flour. Gently knead the dough, sifting in more flour as you knead if the dough is sticky. Knead just until the dough is soft and smooth and slightly tacky.

Divide the dough into 8 pieces. Dust the work surface with a little more flour. Gently roll pieces of dough into long cylinders, ½ inch thick. Cut into pillow-shaped pieces that are ¾–½ inch long.

To shape gnocchi, hold a fork in one hand, convex side of tines facing up. Put the cut edge of a gnocco on the fork against the tines. Using your index finger, gently roll the dough against the tines. This gives a grooved impression on one side and a small depression on the other side from your finger. Dust the fork and your finger with flour as you work.

Bring a large wide pot of water to a gentle simmer. Generously salt the water. Cook the gnocchi in several batches, dropping them into the simmering water and retrieving them with a slotted spoon once they float on the surface for about 10 seconds. Transfer the gnocchi to a warm serving platter as they are done and toss with the melted butter. Serve the gnocchi drizzled with melted butter and grated parmigiano-reggiano.

TURKEY NECK SUGO
makes 3–4 cups

You can buy (or order in advance) packages of turkey necks at your supermarket. They are very inexpensive and add a wonderful rich dark-meat flavor to this subtle sauce, perfect to serve with our homemade gnocchi.

5 pounds turkey necks
Salt and pepper
¼ cup olive oil
2 yellow onions, finely chopped
1 carrot, peeled and finely chopped
¼ whole nutmeg, grated
Pinch of crushed red pepper flakes

2 bay leaves
1 cup whole milk
1 cup white wine
1 can Italian San Marzano plum tomatoes, 28-ounce
Freshly cooked Gnocchi (page 54)
Grated parmigiano-reggiano

Season the turkey necks with salt and pepper. Heat the olive oil in a large, heavy ovenproof pot with a lid over medium-high heat. Put the necks in the pot and brown on all sides, about 20 minutes. Remove the necks from the pot and set them aside.

Reduce heat to medium. Put the onions and carrots into the pot and cook until softened, about 15 minutes. Stir in the nutmeg, red pepper flakes, and bay leaves and season with salt and pepper. Cook for about a minute.

Preheat the oven to 300°. Increase heat to high and add the milk to the pot. Cook, stirring occasionally, until the milk has reduced and been absorbed by the onions and carrots, 5–10 minutes. Add the wine and cook until it has also reduced and been absorbed by the vegetables, 5–10 minutes.

Return the necks to the pot, add the tomatoes, crushing them with your hand, and 4 cups water. Cover the pot and cook in the oven for about 3 hours. Remove the pot from the oven. Remove and discard the necks from the sauce. If the sauce needs further reduction, cook over medium heat, stirring from time to time with a wooden spoon, until it is the consistency that you like. Serve with gnocchi and sprinkle with parmigiano-reggiano.

SIMPLEST TOMATO SAUCE

This is our all-purpose tomato sauce—it's quickly made and we always have the ingredients on hand. Use it to sauce everything from stuffed pasta dishes to gnocchi when you want the delicate dumplings to shine through.

Pour a 28-ounce can crushed tomatoes into a heavy medium pot. Rinse the can with a little water and add it to the pot. Add 1 halved medium yellow onion, 1 crushed clove garlic, 4–6 tablespoons butter, and 2 tablespoons extra-virgin olive oil, then season with salt and pepper.

Simmer over medium-low heat, stirring occasionally, until the onions are soft and the sauce thickens a bit, 30–60 minutes. Adjust the seasonings and add a little more butter to soften and round out the acidity of the sauce, if necessary. A pinch or two of sugar can also help to balance the flavors. Remove and discard the onions and garlic before using. —— *makes about 4 cups*

SIMPLE TOMATO-PANCETTA SAUCE

We use pancetta to enrich this light tomato sauce, but a hunk of prosciutto would do nicely as well.

Put 2 tablespoons extra-virgin olive oil, 1 quartered 8-ounce piece pancetta, 1 chopped yellow onion, and 2 crushed cloves garlic into a heavy medium pot. Cover and sweat the onions over medium-low heat, stirring occasionally, until soft, 15–20 minutes. Open 2 cans (28-ounce size) whole peeled plum tomatoes and crush them with your hand as you add them to the pot, along with their juices. Rinse the cans with 3 cups water, adding the liquid to the pot. Simmer the sauce over medium-low heat, stirring occasionally, until reduced by about half, 1–1½ hours.

Remove and discard the pancetta and either pass the sauce through a food mill or pulse the sauce a few times in a food processor. Strain it back into the pot, discarding the solids. Simmer the sauce over medium heat until reduced by about one-third to a nice, loose saucy consistency, about 30 minutes. Season with salt and pepper. Serve with Gnocchi (page 54) or cooked pasta. —— *makes about 4 cups*

TRUFFLED LOBSTER WITH GNOCCHI
serves 4

There are only three things you have to like to enjoy this sumptuous dish—sweet meaty lobster, velvety rich cream, and earthy black truffle. The tender little pillows of potato gnocchi are an added bonus.

Two 1¼-pound lobsters
Salt
6 tablespoons butter
1 small clove garlic, crushed
1 small dried red chile or 2 pinches dried red pepper flakes
¼ cup white wine

Freshly grated nutmeg
3 cups heavy cream
Pepper
1 fresh black winter truffle, thinly sliced
½ recipe freshly cooked Gnocchi (page 54)

Plunge the tip of a large sharp knife into the heads of the lobsters just behind the eyes. Drop the lobsters head first into a large pot of salted boiling water over high heat and cook for 10 minutes. Use tongs to transfer them from the pot to a colander to let rest until they are cool enough to handle.

Working over a bowl to catch any juices, crack the lobster shells and remove the meat from the tail, knuckles, and claws, reserving the shells and any juices. Cut the lobster meat into large bite-size pieces, leaving the claw meat whole.

Melt the butter in a large, wide, heavy pot over medium-low heat. Add the garlic, dried chile, lobster shells, wine, and a generous grating of nutmeg. Cover and sweat the shells, stirring occasionally, for 15–20 minutes. Add the cream and any accumulated lobster juices from the bowl and season with salt and pepper. Gently simmer until the cream is impregnated with the flavors from the lobster, 5–10 minutes.

Strain the lobster cream through a fine sieve into a heavy medium pot, discarding the solids. Add the truffle slices and the lobster meat to the cream and gently simmer over medium-low heat until the lobster is warmed through, 5–10 minutes. Adjust the seasonings.

Divide the warm gnocchi and the pieces of lobster between four warm deep plates or wide soup bowls. Spoon the truffles and cream over each serving and garnish with a little fresh tarragon, if you like.

WHOLE POT-ROASTED CHICKEN WITH GNOCCHI
serves 6

This is the chicken to make when you're after the flavor of a moist roasted bird with crisp skin, but want more juices than are typically released when roasting it in a pan. Adding a bit of water to the chicken as you roast it in a heavy covered pot (a deep enameled cast-iron one does the trick) produces plenty of juicy broth. It's rich enough that should you have leftovers, you're guaranteed a lovely lunch the next day of cold chicken with a delicious gelée.

1 whole chicken, 3–5 pounds
2 tablespoons butter, softened
2 tablespoons extra-virgin olive oil
Salt and pepper
3 sprigs fresh sage

4 medium carrots, peeled and sliced into rounds
1 recipe freshly cooked Gnocchi (page 54)

Preheat the oven to 375°. Rinse the chicken and pat it dry with paper towels. Rub the chicken all over with the butter and put it into a heavy pot that the chicken fits into easily with the lid on. Rub the chicken with the olive oil and season with salt and pepper. Put the sage into the pot with the chicken along with 2 cups water.

Cover the pot and transfer it to the oven. Roast the chicken for 30 minutes for a 3–4-pound bird; 45 minutes for a 4–5-pound bird. Remove the pot from the oven. Baste the chicken with the brothy juices. Add the carrots to the pot, scattering them around the chicken. Return the pot to the oven, uncovered, and finish roasting the chicken until golden brown on top and the juices run clear when you pierce the thigh with a sharp knife, about 15 minutes.

Remove the chicken from the pot and let rest for 10 minutes before carving. Season the brothy juices with salt and pepper. Serve the chicken and warm gnocchi together in wide bowls with the carrots and broth spooned on top.

GREEN & WHITE SOUP WITH GNOCCHI
serves 6–8

This versatile soup, our green and white version of a minestrone, can be made with other leafy greens like spinach or coarsely chopped escarole. And short pasta or cooked dried white beans can be used in place of the gnocchi. To preserve its fresh green color, prepare the soup the day you plan to eat it.

1 large bunch white-stemmed
   Swiss chard

3 tablespoons butter

1 tablespoon extra-virgin olive oil

1 medium yellow onion, chopped

1 clove garlic, thinly sliced

Salt and pepper

3–4 medium zucchini, quartered
   lengthwise, thickly sliced crosswise

8 cups rich, flavorful chicken stock

1 bunch fresh parsley, leaves
   coarsely chopped

1 recipe freshly cooked Gnocchi
   (page 54)

Parmigiano-reggiano

Trim off the chard stems from their long leaves. Slice the stems and coarsely chop the leaves, setting them aside in separate piles.

Melt the butter and olive oil together in a heavy medium pot over medium-low heat. Add the chard stems, the onions, and garlic. Cover the pot and cook, stirring occasionally, until the vegetables are soft, 15–20 minutes. Stir in the chard leaves and season to taste with salt and pepper. Cover and cook until the leaves wilt. Add the zucchini and stock, bring to a boil over medium-high heat, then reduce the heat to medium. Simmer the soup until the vegetables are tender, about 45 minutes. Adjust the seasonings. Add the parsley just before serving.

Divide the warm gnocchi between 6–8 warm soup bowls and ladle some of the soup into each bowl. Garnish each with some shaved parmigiano-reggiano, if you like.

Eat Your Vegetables

NILOUFER'S CAULIFLOWER & CHICKPEAS
serves 4–6

We know we have mentioned Niloufer Ichaporia King's book, *My Bombay Kitchen* (University of California Press, 2007) before, but actually we can't mention it enough. While our cooking tends toward the fresh herb–based, she really understands spices. We called her late one night when we were noodling around with some cauliflower recipes and off the top of her lovely head this is what she told us to do. Niloufer is a giver and generously shares her deep culinary knowledge. Lucky for all of us.

2 tablespoons ghee, clarified butter, or canola oil
½ teaspoon fennel seeds
1 small yellow onion, minced
2 tablespoons grated, peeled fresh ginger
2–3 cloves garlic, minced into a paste
½ teaspoon turmeric
¼ teaspoon cayenne, or more

1 teaspoon garam masala
Salt
2 cups cooked chickpeas
1 head cauliflower, broken in florets
Large handful cilantro, leaves and stems chopped
Juice of 1 lime

Heat the ghee in a large skillet over medium heat and toast the fennel seeds for about 1 minute. Add the onion, ginger, and garlic and cook, stirring and scraping the bottom of the skillet with a wooden spoon to keep it from sticking, until brown, about 10 minutes.

Add the turmeric, cayenne, garam masala, and a big pinch of salt to the skillet and cook, dribbling in a little water as you stir. Add the chickpeas, cauliflower, and ½ cup water. Cover and cook until the cauliflower is tender, 15–20 minutes. Add the chopped cilantro and lime juice and serve with yogurt and rice or big floppy flatbread like chapatis, if you like.

THE APPLE FARM'S ROASTED CAULIFLOWER

At the Philo Apple Farm's cooking school, Karen Bates says they sometimes use olive oil, fresh lemon juice, or thinly sliced Meyer lemons if they are short on preserved lemons.

Preheat the oven to 400°. Divide one whole cauliflower into florets and toss with 4 tablespoons melted butter and 3 tablespoons finely chopped preserved lemon. Roast until tender, about 20 minutes. Season with salt and pepper. —— *serves 4–6*

WARM SAVOY CABBAGE SALAD
serves 8

This warm salad is a classic of the Alsace region. Even if it seems slightly weird to mix Japanese with Alsatian, we prefer rice wine vinegar's slightly sweet mellow flavor to traditional white wine vinegar's sharp bite. This dish is a delicious counterpoint to rich meats like goose or ham.

8 pieces thick-sliced bacon,
    sliced into thin pieces

1 cup rice wine vinegar

1 apple, peeled, cored, and chopped

1 savoy cabbage, cored,
    leaves julienned

Salt and pepper

Fry the bacon in a large heavy pot, stirring from time to time over medium heat until it is crisp and brown, about 20 minutes. Keep the heat low so the fat doesn't burn and take on an unpleasant taste. Lift the bacon from the pot with a slotted spatula and drain on paper towels.

Pour the vinegar into the pot with the bacon fat and cook for a minute over medium heat. Add the apples and cabbage, and season with salt and pepper. Cook until wilted and tender, about 30 minutes. Taste and adjust seasoning (don't hold back on the pepper, this dish benefits from its spicy bite). Transfer to a serving bowl and sprinkle with the bacon. Serve warm or at room temperature.

RED CABBAGE WITH APPLES & CHESTNUTS
serves 6–8

Cabbage hasn't been on our radar for a while. Let's face it, it does have a rather gassy reputation, and it seems to have gone right out of fashion. But our fall markets are filled with piles of ruffled Savoy, long crinkled Napa, and good old green and beautiful red cabbages and this year we couldn't resist them. They all looked so pretty and fresh that we had a cabbage-fest, cooking them every which way, and now we can't get enough of them.

One of our favorite recipes is this red cabbage cooked with chestnuts and apples—a classic dish of Alsace. In fact, the region's Christmas goose (which is something like ours—see page 94) is traditionally served on a bed of red cabbage with chestnuts. We even found an old Alsatian recipe in Elizabeth David's 1962 culinary odyssey, *French Provincial Cooking*, that calls for filling a whole head of cabbage with chestnuts and bacon. Those Alsatians sure know their way around the *Brassica* family. They often add vinegar and sugar to red cabbage for a piquant flavor. We add the best Riesling we can afford instead, and sip along as the cabbage cooks.

2 tablespoons duck fat or canola oil	1 head red cabbage, cored and sliced into strips
1 large onion, thinly sliced	1 cup Riesling
Salt and pepper	2 green apples, peeled and cubed
Bay leaf	One 14-ounce jar roasted chestnuts
Juice of 1 small lemon	

Melt the fat in a large heavy pot over medium-high heat. Add the onions and sauté until they are soft, about 5 minutes. Season liberally with salt and pepper. Add the bay leaf and lemon juice and stir with a wooden spoon to mix everything together.

Add the cabbage and Riesling and stir to mix. Reduce the heat to low, cover, and gently simmer for about 30 minutes. Add apples and chestnuts and stir to mix, taking care to keep the chestnuts whole. Cover and cook until the cabbage is very tender, about 30 minutes.

PURÉED CELERY ROOT & POTATOES
serves 4

Celery root hardly makes your heart flutter when you see it in the market—quite the opposite. But peel that big, dirty, tough-looking orb and you reveal pale flesh with a fine delicate flavor somewhere between celery and parsley. For a refined purée, push the vegetables through a sieve once you've riced them. If you prefer a more rustic dish, just mash everything together with a fork. Either way, whisk in the flavorful cooking broth rather than milk or cream—it will deepen the celery flavor.

1 large celery root, about 1 pound, peeled and cut into very small cubes

2 russet potatoes, peeled and cubed

Salt

4 tablespoons butter, cut in pieces

Freshly grated nutmeg

Pepper

Put the celery root and potato in a medium pot and add enough water to cover by ½ inch. Add a big pinch of salt. Cover, and bring to a boil over medium heat. Reduce the heat to keep the water at a gentle boil and cook until the celery root and potatoes are very tender, about 30 minutes. Strain, and reserve the cooking liquid.

Push the vegetables through a ricer or food mill back into the pot. Add the butter (reserving a little for the top) and stir with a wooden spoon. Add a big pinch of nutmeg and season with salt and pepper. Add the cooking liquid a tablespoon at a time, whisking until smooth and creamy. For a very smooth purée, push through a fine-mesh sieve. Transfer to a gratin dish, dot the top with the reserved butter, and keep warm in a low oven.

COLLARDS & BACON
serves 4

Of all the long-cooked greens, we love collards the best. Those big leathery leaves cook down into such sweet suppleness. A Mississippi friend told us stories of her father washing big batches of greens in their bathtub, rinsing and rinsing and rinsing, to wash away all the sandy dirt trapped in the leaves. But the collards that we buy at the market come soil-free, so a simple rinse in the sink will do it.

You might start out with a big pot full of leaves, but as they cook and release their lovely pot liquor they will reduce considerably. A bowl of these with a piece of cornbread or a slice of toasted country bread is a perfect lunch or supper.

1 big bunch collard greens	1 garlic clove, sliced
1 cup chopped slab bacon	Salt and pepper
1 large onion, thinly sliced	Really good extra-virgin olive oil

Rinse all the collard leaves under running water in the sink. Don't dry the leaves, just shake off the water as you go. Folding each leaf in half lengthwise (as if you were closing a book), cut out and discard the center rib and stem. Slice the leaves crosswise into thin ribbons.

Put the bacon into a large heavy pot and cook over medium heat until it releases some of its fat. Add the onions and garlic and season with salt and pepper. Cook for a few minutes to just soften the onions a bit. Add the wet collards, reduce the heat to low, cover, and cook until the greens are very soft and swimming in their pot liquor, about 2 hours. Season with salt and pepper to taste. Serve drizzled with olive oil.

Cauliflower soufflé

CAULIFLOWER SOUFFLÉ
serves 4

Sally Schmitt makes this gorgeous soufflé for her cooking classes in her big, pretty kitchen on The Apple Farm in Philo, California. We've learned lots about cooking and eating from the Schmitts, but it's "the good life" they have on their beautiful family farm that truly inspires us.

FOR THE SOUFFLÉ
5 tablespoons salted butter
3 tablespoons finely grated parmigiano-reggiano
2 cups Roasted Cauliflower (page 65), finely chopped
¼ cup finely chopped parsley

Salt and white pepper
¼ cup all-purpose flour
1½ cups whole milk
6 large egg yolks
8 large egg whites

FOR THE BROWN BUTTER
8 tablespoons (1 stick) salted butter

For the soufflé, preheat oven to 400° with a rack set in the middle. Use 1 tablespoon softened butter to grease a 2-quart soufflé dish, then sprinkle with cheese, knocking out excess.

Mix together the cauliflower, parsley, and salt and pepper to taste, in a large bowl.

Melt remaining 4 tablespoons butter in a heavy medium saucepan over medium heat. Whisk in flour, then cook, whisking, until pale golden, about 2 minutes. Season with salt and pepper. Add the milk a little at a time, whisking constantly until very smooth and thick. Remove from heat and whisk in the yolks, one at a time. Stir into the cauliflower mixture.

Beat the whites in a bowl with an electric mixer at high speed until they just hold stiff peaks (they should not look dry). Stir a heaping spoonful of whites into the cauliflower to lighten it, then gently fold in remaining whites until just combined. Gently spoon into soufflé dish (leave at least 1½ inches of space at top) and bake until golden brown and top appears set, 35–40 minutes.

For the brown butter, cook butter in a small heavy saucepan over medium heat, stirring occasionally, until it turns golden with a nutlike fragrance and the flecks on bottom of the pan are rich brown, about 6 minutes. Remove from heat.

Serve the soufflé while it is still all puffy, drizzled with warm brown butter.

fins 'n' things

SOLE & SHRIMP
serves 4

When my daughters were little we lived for a time in a beautiful old building high on top of one of San Francisco's famous hills. My brother, my Aunt Cele and Uncle Warde, and my young family had apartments there. Often, we all ate together and since I was hungry to learn my way around the kitchen, I watched all my aunt's moves—she was a wonderful, simple, and stylish cook. Cele marketed every day; I think she liked the social aspect of her errands. She would pull on her gloves, a smart coat, and with a quick wave to my uncle, off she'd skip down Washington Street's steep hill to Polk Street to buy what she needed for dinner that evening. If we were lucky it would be petrale sole and bay shrimp—simple and stylish. Now I live on the East Coast so I cook grey sole and the smallest shrimp I can find to relive the flavor of those fun family meals. — CH

4 sole filets, about 4 ounces each	½ pound small shrimp, peeled
Salt and pepper	and split in two lengthwise
½ cup flour	Juice of 1 lemon
8 tablespoons salted butter	¼ cup heavy cream, optional

Pat the fish filets dry with a paper towel and season to taste with salt and pepper. Dredge the filets in the flour and shake off any excess.

Melt 2 tablespoons of the butter in a large skillet over medium-high heat until foaming. Slide 2 filets into the skillet. Cook the fish in batches so that you have room to turn them over without breaking them into pieces. Brown the fish about 2 minutes per side and use a large fish spatula to turn the filets. Transfer the cooked fish to a warm platter. Repeat with the remaining filets.

Melt 1 tablespoon of the butter in the skillet over medium-high heat, add the shrimp and season with salt and pepper. Cook until the shrimp have turned an opaque pink color, 3–5 minutes. Transfer them to the platter with the fish.

Melt remaining 3 tablespoons of butter in a small skillet over medium-high heat, swirling the pan until the butter is foaming and pale gold. Whisk in lemon juice then pour over shrimp and sole. Or if you like, add cream and cook until sauce bubbles and thickens. Garnish with fresh tarragon or another herb that you like.

LOBSTER WITH BROWNED CREAM
serves 2

Once, long ago, I ate at a little seaside restaurant in Normandy—its name and exact location, sadly, have drifted right out of my head. It was a casual place with no menu: the waiter simply recited the day's offerings. My French was spotty, so I just said *"oui"* when I heard *"spécialité de la maison."* I don't remember the first course—most likely it was a dozen briny belons. But then the waiter brought a whole lobster split in two, both halves filled with a golden mousse of thick cream enveloping all that sweet meat. *That* I'll never forget! To replicate Normandy cream, use the thickest (ideally 35% butterfat), most "natural" cream you can find. ——CH

1 lobster, 2 pounds
Salt
¼–½ cup heavy cream

1 tablespoon cold butter,
   cut into small pieces
Pepper

Plunge the lobster head first into a large pot of salted boiling water over high heat. Cook for 3 minutes then use tongs to remove the lobster from the pot and allow to drain on several thicknesses of paper towel.

When the lobster is cool enough to handle, split it lengthwise with a large heavy knife, taking care not to sever your artery! Cut through the back splitting the head and body in two. Continue to cut through the tail with the knife or a strong pair of kitchen shears. Separate the halves and place them meat side up in a baking pan. Remove and discard the stomach sac between the eyes. Cover the claws with a towel and use the handle of the knife to crack them open on the top side. Remove the pieces of cracked shells.

Pour the cream into the two lobster halves, around and over the meat in the tail, into the body, and into the cracked claws. Use as much cream as the lobster will accept. Tuck the pieces of butter into the claw and body and tail pieces. Season with salt and pepper.

Preheat the broiler. Put the pan with lobster under the hot broiler and cook until the cream is bubbling and brown, 7–10 minutes. Transfer the lobster to two plates, taking care not to spill out the delicious juices. Serve with crusty bread to sop up the cream.

STEAMED MUSSELS WITH POTATOES
serves 2

We had the pleasure of working with Italian cooking authority and cookbook author Julia della Croce at Canal House while photographing her most recent book, *Italian Comfort Food* (Kyle Books, 2010). One of the last dishes we prepared together before the shoot was over called for little square cubes of potato. Rather than discarding the trimmings, someone put them into a small tub of water and stuck them in the fridge—the perfect thing to take up room in the cramped space just to be thrown away two weeks later. A couple of days passed, and looking to make something for lunch, I went rummaging around in the refrigerator and found a bag of fresh mussels. Okay. Steamed open, they'd make a nice meal, but not quite enough to satisfy our hunger. Rooting around some more, I discovered the tub of potato trimmings. What if I added them to the pot with the mussels? How bad could that be? Well, by now you know the end of the story. Steamed together—the mussel broth soaking into the tender scraps of potato; the potatoes giving body to the flavorful broth—the dish was a revelation, yet obvious in hindsight. No matter. It's so delicious we now have a hard time preparing steamed mussels any other way. —— MH

1 russet potato, peeled, halved
  lengthwise, and sliced
1½ cups dry white wine
2 pounds mussels, debearded
4 tablespoons butter, cut into pieces
1–2 cloves garlic, thinly sliced

Rind from ¼ preserved lemon,
  chopped
Salt and pepper
2–3 tablespoons extra-virgin olive oil
1 bunch fresh parsley, leaves chopped

Put potatoes, wine, and 1 cup of water into a heavy medium pot. Cover and boil over medium-high heat until the potatoes begin to soften, about 5 minutes. Add the mussels, butter, garlic, and preserved lemon. Season with salt and pepper. Cover and steam mussels, stirring occasionally, until the potatoes are tender and breaking apart and the mussels open, 8–10 minutes.

Remove from heat. Drizzle in the oil and add the parsley. Spoon the mussels, potatoes, and broth into big warm bowls. Discard any shells that don't open.

CHOWDER
serves 6–8

Chowder came to this country with the Pilgrims. They cooked what they had—salt pork and plenty of cod (they named a whole cape after it!), adding potatoes and onions if they had them. We've spiced up our soup with a few Spanish embellishments. Take care not to add too much salt; the crisp salt pork that you add at the end will season the soup.

10 ounces salt pork, diced small
1 large onion, finely chopped
Pinch of saffron
2 bay leaves
Pepper

6–8 white potatoes, peeled and cut in large pieces
2 quarts flavorful fish stock
1½ pounds cod filet, cut in 6–8 pieces
Pinch of pimentón

Put the salt pork in a large heavy pot and cook over medium heat, stirring occasionally so the pieces brown on all sides, about 15 minutes. Use a slotted spatula to transfer to a paper towel–lined plate. Pour off and discard all but about 2 tablespoons of the rendered fat in the pot.

Add the onions, saffron, bay leaves, and a few grinds of pepper to the pot. Cook, stirring from time to time, until the onions have softened but not browned, about 20 minutes. Add the potatoes and the fish stock, cover, and cook until potatoes are soft, about 15 minutes.

Add the cod and cook for about 10 minutes. (Don't stir too much, you want to keep the fish in large pieces.) Taste and adjust seasonings. Remove the bay leaves. Ladle the chowder into bowls and divide the salt pork between the bowls. Sprinkle with pimentón and fresh herbs, if you like.

sausages

·෬· MAKING HOMEMADE FRESH SAUSAGES ·෬·

We are huge fans of chef Paul Bertolli, founder of Fra Mani Handcrafted Salumi. His book, *Cooking by Hand* (Clarkson Potter, 2003), is our bible for making sausages. Over the years we've learned so much from him. Here are our CliffsNotes of his sausage-making advice:

Traditionally, hogs were slaughtered in December and that's when all the sausage making was done. Meat and fat are easier to finely chop or grind when very cold, almost frozen. So when mixing the chopped meat and fat, keep everything very cold over an ice water bath, that way there is less chance of it all getting too warm and soft—"smearing"—which can make the finished sausages dry and crumbly.

Unless you have a professional-meat grinder, finely hand-chop the cold meat and fat with a very sharp knife or cleaver. The dread "smear" can be caused by the heat generated by friction from hand-crank and electric mixer meat grinders. Use the meat grinder only for stuffing the sausage meat into the casings, first fitting it with the stuffing attachment.

To make juicy sausages you need the right ratio of fat to meat. We like to use a ratio of approximately 30 percent fat to 70 percent lean meat.

BOILED PORK SKIN ·෬· The boiled skin will enhance both the texture and the flavor of the sausages. Remove the skin from 1½ pounds fatback. Cut it into strips and cook it in a pot of gently boiling water over medium-high heat until swollen and tender, about 40 minutes. Drain, rinse, and set aside.

ITALIAN SAUSAGE
makes about 20

Small tub 1¼-inch natural hog casings
2 pounds boneless pork butt, cubed
10 ounces fatback, cubed
8 ounces boiled fresh pork skin (page 82), cubed
2 cloves garlic, finely minced

1 tablespoon plus 1 teaspoon kosher salt
1 tablespoon ground black pepper
2 teaspoons ground anise seeds
2 teaspoons ground fennel seeds
1 teaspoon sugar

1. CASINGS ·◦· Soak several lengths of hog casings in a medium bowl of cold water until soft and pliable, about 1 hour. Then slip one end of a length of casing onto the kitchen faucet and run cold water through it for a minute or so to rinse out any salt. Repeat with the remaining casings. Return rinsed casings to the bowl and cover with cold water.

2. CHOPPING ·◦· Using a very sharp knife, mince the meat, put it in a large stainless steel mixing bowl, and put it in the refrigerator. Finely dice the fatback, then the pork skin. Add them to the bowl with the meat.

3. MIXING ·◦· Set the bowl with the meat into another bowl filled with ice and water (an ice bath). Add the garlic, salt, pepper, anise, fennel, sugar, and ¼ cup ice-cold water to the meat. Mix everything together with a stiff rubber spatula, using a cutting and folding motion, making sure that the meat stays very cold. It will become sticky and leave a whitish film on the sides of the bowl.

4. STUFFING ·◦· Secure a hand-crank meat grinder to a work table. Be sure that the cutting blade and the perforated plate are removed. Fit the grinder with the sausage stuffing attachment. Cut the casings into 3-foot lengths. Slip the end of a casing onto the nozzle, bunching it up on the nozzle until only 5 inches remain loose at the end. Crank meat evenly through the grinder into the casing, easing the filled casing off the nozzle as you go. Stop stuffing when about 3 inches of the casing remain on the nozzle. Remove the filled casing from the nozzle. Tie a knot at one end.

5. TWISTING AND TYING ·◦· Working from the knotted end, pinch the filled casing to make 3-inch links. Twist at the pinch—right hand toward you, left hand away from you—to form links. Knot the end (or tie with kitchen string). Prick the sausages with a straight pin to release any trapped air. Repeat the process until all the meat has been turned into sausages.

6. STORING ·◦· Lay the sausages out on a kitchen towel–lined tray and refrigerate uncovered, turning them from time to time until their surface feels dry and no longer moist, about 2 hours. Wrap in plastic and refrigerate for up to 3 days, or freeze, well wrapped, for several months.

DUCK SAUSAGE WITH QUATRE ÉPICES
makes about 20

FOR THE QUATRE ÉPICES
1 teaspoon ground white pepper
¼ teaspoon ground nutmeg
¼ teaspoon ground cloves
⅛ teaspoon ground cinnamon
⅛ teaspoon ground ginger

Small tub 1¼-inch natural hog casings

2 pounds boneless skinless duck
  thigh meat, cubed
8 ounces fatback, cubed
8 ounces boiled fresh pork skin
  (page 82), cubed
4 ounces salt pork, cubed
2 teaspoons kosher salt
1 teaspoon sugar

For the quatre épices, mix together the spices in a small bowl and set side.

Follow steps 1 and 2 (page 83), using casings, duck, fatback, pork skin, and salt pork (see above).

Follow step 3 (page 83), replacing seasonings with quatre épices, salt, and sugar (see above).

Follow steps 4 through 6 (page 83).

LAMB SAUSAGE WITH CURRANTS
makes about 20

1 cup dried currants
⅓ cup Cognac
Small tub 1¼-inch natural hog casings
2 pounds boneless leg of lamb, cubed
10 ounces fatback, cubed
8 ounces boiled fresh pork skin
  (page 82), cubed

1 tablespoon plus 1 teaspoon
  kosher salt
1 tablespoon ground black pepper
1 teaspoon sugar
¼ teaspoon cayenne

Soak the currants in the Cognac in a small bowl until plump.

Follow steps 1 and 2 (page 83), using casings, lamb, fatback, and pork skin (see above).

Follow step 3 (page 83), replacing seasonings with currants and Cognac, salt, pepper, sugar, and cayenne (see above).

Follow steps 4 through 6 (page 83).

Facing page, top row: hand-chopping the fatback and meat; rinsing natural hog casings;
bottom row: filling a sausage casing using a meat grinder; twisting and tying sausages

SAUSAGES WITH APPLES & ONIONS
serves 4

We make quick skillet meals like this one of sausages with onions and apples (and sometimes pears) when we are short on time and have either our own fresh sausages on hand or good ones that we buy. Small butcher shops sell wonderful fresh sausages, of course, but when we buy sausages at the grocery store, we get fresh ones from the butcher department rather than the ones that come in the Cryovac packages in the meat case. If the market is good, it usually has a nice selection of fresh sausages.

2 tablespoons olive oil

4 small yellow onions, halved lengthwise

8 fresh sausages, any flavor you like (page 82), pricked

4 small apples, peeled, cored, and quartered

Salt and pepper

Fresh sage, optional

Heat the oil in a large heavy skillet over medium heat. Add the onions cut side down, cover, and cook until just tender and browned on the bottom, about 15 minutes.

Tuck the sausages and apples around the onions in the skillet. Season with salt and pepper. Use two skillets if everything is too crowded together. Cook over medium heat, turning the sausages and apples as they begin to brown, but leaving the onions in place. Take care to leave the onion halves whole. Continue cooking until everything is nicely browned, then reduce the heat to medium-low.

Cover the skillet and cook until the sausages are cooked through and the apples and onions are tender, 5–10 minutes. Adjust seasonings. Serve garnished with fresh sage, if you like.

GRILLED SAUSAGES & QUAIL
serves 4

Any (or all three) of our homemade sausages are delicious with these smoky quail. No time to make sausage? Just use your favorite from the store.

8 whole jumbo quail
1 small bunch fresh thyme
1 small bunch fresh
  rosemary

3–4 tablespoons really good
  extra-virgin olive oil
Salt and pepper
8 fresh sausages, any flavor
  you like (page 82), pricked

Rinse the quail and pat dry with paper towels. Put the birds into a dish and rub all over with the herbs, olive oil, and lots of salt and pepper. Marinate for 1–2 hours.

Prepare a hot hardwood charcoal or gas grill. Grill the quail with the herb bunches and the sausages over hot coals, turning them when they are well browned and the birds are a little charred in places. Remove the herbs before they char. Move the sausages to a cooler spot on the grill if there are flare-ups. Grill the quail and sausages until they are deeply browned all over and the meat is just cooked through, 5–15 minutes depending on the heat of your grill.

Put the sausages and quail together on a warm platter, drizzle with a little olive oil, and season with a bit of salt. Serve with polenta, if you like.

POLENTA

We serve big spoonfuls of this buttery polenta with our Grilled Sausages & Quail (page 89). We prepare it while the quail marinate and the charcoal is getting hot. When it's done, we put a couple tablespoons of butter on top to prevent a crust from forming on the surface (stir it in before serving).

Put 5 cups cold water into a medium, heavy-bottomed pot. Stir in 1 cup polenta and 2 generous pinches of salt. Bring to a boil over medium-high heat, stirring often. Reduce the heat to medium-low and cook the polenta, stirring often, until it is tender, 45–60 minutes. The polenta will swell and thicken as it cooks. Stir in a little more water as needed to keep it loose until it has finished cooking. Stir in 4 tablespoons butter and season with salt and pepper. —— *serves 4*

CASSOULET OUR WAY
serves 4–6

When we don't have our own confit of goose (or duck) to use for this simple cassoulet, we buy it already prepared from the market or we mail order it.

1 pound dried white beans, soaked
4 tablespoons goose, duck, or
   chicken fat, or butter
8 fresh pork, lamb, or duck sausages
   (page 82), pricked
1 yellow onion, finely chopped
2 cloves garlic, finely chopped
Confit of 2 whole goose or 4 whole

duck legs, cut at the joint into
   legs and thighs
1 large bunch fresh thyme
2 bay leaves
3 quarts chicken stock
Salt and pepper
2 tablespoons butter
1 cup fresh bread crumbs

Put the beans into a heavy medium pot. Cover with cold water. Bring to a boil, then simmer over medium-low until tender, about 1 hour. Drain.

Preheat the oven to 350°. Heat the goose fat in a large, heavy ovenproof pot with a lid over medium heat. Brown the sausages all over, about 5 minutes. Transfer to a plate and set aside. Add the onions and garlic to the pot and cook until soft, about 5 minutes. Add half the cooked beans to the pot. Arrange the sausages and goose legs on the beans. Add the thyme and bay leaves, and cover with remaining beans. Add stock to cover the beans by about 1 inch. Season with salt and pepper. Cover the pot and bake the cassoulet for 1 hour.

Melt butter in a skillet over medium heat. Toast the bread crumbs until golden, about 5 minutes. Remove cassoulet from the oven, sprinkle with bread crumbs, and return it to oven, uncovered. Bake until browned on top, 15–30 minutes.

CONFIT OF GOOSE LEGS

Preheat oven to 250°. Melt 8–10 cups rendered goose fat in a deep, heavy pot over low heat. Remove pot from heat. Slip 4 whole goose legs into the warm fat. The legs should be submerged. Add 1 bay leaf to the pot. Transfer the pot to the oven and gently cook the legs until they are very tender, about 3 hours. Transfer the legs, bay leaf, and fat to a deep bowl, crock, or pot, making sure the legs are completely submerged in the fat. Cover and refrigerate the confit of goose for at least 2 days or up to 3 months. The flavor improves with time.——*makes 4*

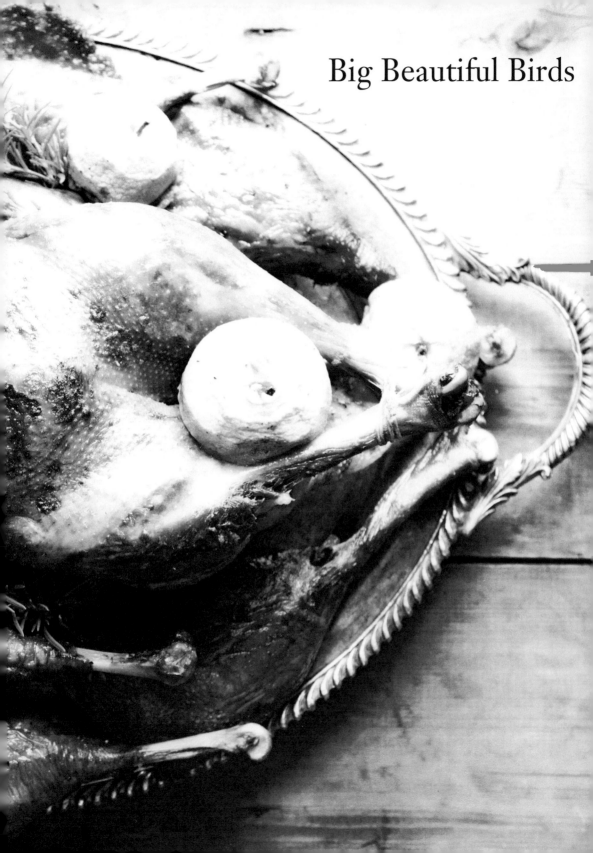

ROAST GOOSE WITH TEN LEGS
serves 10–12

Howard Helmer is one of the great characters of the food world, with his dapper duds, his great smile, and his irrepressible giggle. A spokesperson for both the American Egg Board and Schiltz Goose Farm, he holds the Guinness World Record for the "World's Fastest Omelette Maker". Every year around the holidays, Howard hires a big black Town Car and fills the trunk with frozen geese. He zooms around Manhattan delivering these birds to all the lucky food editors. When we were editors we were on that list. He'd hurry into our offices laughing, "Hello, hello", and hand each of us a big frozen goose, and then off he'd zip. It's thanks to Howard that we are such aficionados of this glorious bird.

While a whole golden goose makes a beautiful presentation, the legs are where you find the real meat and delicious flavor. Schiltz Goose Farm, in South Dakota, sells beautiful big birds and also whole legs, four to the package. We roast one big bird for the tah-dah factor, along with 8 legs—and everyone is happy and well fed.

1 whole goose, 8–10 pounds	3 tablespoons juniper berries, crushed
Salt and pepper	
1 large handful fresh thyme leaves	8 whole goose legs (thigh and drumstick attached)

Preheat the oven to 400°. Remove the neck and giblets from the goose and save to make stock, if you like. Remove any excess fat and save to make rendered fat, if you like. Rinse and pat the goose dry with paper towels. Use a wooden spoon to mix and crush together 1 tablespoon salt, 2 teaspoons pepper, the thyme leaves, and juniper berries in a small bowl. Rub the bird inside and out with the mixture, and also on the goose legs. Use a sharp fork to prick the goose and the legs all over to release fat while they cook. Bend the wings behind the bird's back and tie its legs together.

Put the goose on a rack in a roasting pan. Pour 1 cup water into the pan to keep the fat from burning. Arrange the 8 legs in a single layer in another

Overleaf: Roast Goose with Ten Legs

large roasting pan and add a little water. Cover both pans with foil and roast for 45 minutes. Reduce the temperature to 325°, uncover both pans and roast until a meat thermometer inserted into a thigh registers 180°and the skin is brown and crisp, 1–2 hours. If the legs are cooked before the goose, remove them from the oven. You can pop them back in for a few minutes to warm them before serving. Season with salt and pepper.

Transfer the goose along with the legs to a large platter and serve with Apples Cooked with Cumin (page 95).

APPLES COOKED WITH CUMIN
makes 10

These fragrant apples are a delicious accompaniment for Roast Goose with Ten Legs but they are also delicious with Fresh Ham with Madeira Sauce (page 102) and Roasted Pork Belly (page 106). Fall is the season for apples and we are lucky to have beautiful orchards all around us. Branch out and try an heirloom variety that is a cooking apple. The apples will hold their shape but have a nice tender texture. You can make this recipe using fewer apples but don't cut down on the butter, sugar, and cumin.

8 tablespoons (1 stick) butter
1 tablespoon ground cumin
2 tablespoons sugar

10 whole apples such as Winesap, Empire, or Braeburn, peeled and cored

Melt the butter over medium heat in an large pan with a lid. Add the cumin and sugar, then add the apples. Cook, basting and turning the apples to coat them in the butter. Reduce heat to low, cover, and cook, basting from time to time, until they are tender, about 1 hour.

CHICKEN & MUSHROOMS
serves 8

Alice Waters once told us that her dear friend Martine could feed nine people with one chicken. With the meaty 6- to 8-pound chickens we buy from our local farmer, we can do the same thing.

One 6–8-pound chicken, or two
  3-pound chickens
Salt and pepper
Wondra or all-purpose flour
8 tablespoons (1 stick) butter
1 large onion, thickly sliced

2 cloves garlic, minced
2 cups Riesling
24 ounces button mushrooms or
  wild mushroom, sliced
Juice of 1 lemon
2 cups heavy cream or crème fraîche

Cut the chicken into 16 pieces; 6 pieces of breast, 4 pieces of thigh, 2 legs, 4 pieces of wings. (If you are using 2 chickens, cut each into 8 pieces.) Lay chicken pieces on a cutting board, season with salt and pepper and a light dusting of flour. Turn the pieces over, season and dust with flour.

Melt 2 tablespoons of the butter in each of two large skillets over medium-high heat. Divide the chicken between the skillets by dark and light meat. Brown the chicken on all sides for about 15 minutes. Add half the onions and garlic to each skillet and cook for a few minutes. Reduce the heat to low, then add 1 cup Riesling to each skillet. Cover each skillet loosely with a piece of foil and cook until the juices run clear when the chicken is pieced with a sharp knife, about 45 minutes. (The white meat may only take 30 minutes to cook so keep an eye on it.) Transfer the cooked chicken and onions to a large platter and keep warm in a very low oven. Use a rubber spatula and transfer all the pan juices from both skillets to a small bowl.

Melt the remaining 4 tablespoons of butter in one of the skillets over medium-high heat. Add the mushrooms, toss in the butter and cook until lightly browned, about 15 minutes. Add the lemon juice and season with salt and pepper. Use a slotted spoon to transfer the mushrooms on top of the chicken. Stir the pan juices into the skillet over medium heat. Add the cream and stir until hot and bubbly. Pour through a strainer over the chicken. Serve garnished with herbs, if you like.

TRUFFLED CHICKEN
serves 4–6

In the French classic, *poulet demi-deuil*—chicken in half-mourning—fresh black winter truffles are slipped between the skin and flesh of a chicken. The bird is then refrigerated for several days for the flesh to "truffle". Traditionally, the chicken is poached and "half-mourning" refers to the black of the truffle against the white of the skin and flesh. We roast the chicken for our version of this famous dish.

Fresh black winter truffles, *Tuber melanosporum*, are found primarily in France's Périgord and Provence regions during late fall and winter months. Exported all over the world, their price varies with the abundance of the foragers' harvest and what the market will bear—but they sell for big money. The flavor of a quality fresh black truffle, like sex, is hard to describe, yet its taste is so fundamentally good that even if you know nothing about them, your whole body will recognize the experience and know what to do. Eating a truffle involves all your senses, and then some. So just close your eyes and go with the feeling.

1 chicken, 5 pounds	Salt and pepper
4 tablespoons softened butter	1 cup white wine, your favorite
1 or more fresh black winter truffles, thinly sliced	1 cup heavy cream

Use your fingers to loosen the skin of the chicken from the breast and legs, taking care not to tear the skin. Rub butter under skin all over the flesh. Slip truffle slices under the skin, covering as much of the flesh as you can. Wrap chicken with plastic and refrigerate for up to 2 days, allowing time for the truffle to perfume the bird's flesh.

Preheat oven to 400°. Unwrap chicken and season with salt and pepper. Put in a heavy ovenproof pot with a lid. Pour wine into pot. Cover and roast for 1 hour.

Remove from oven. Gather your dining companions around you, lift the cover off the pot, and inhale the sweet truffly perfume. Transfer bird to a cutting board and allow it to rest while you make the sauce. Pour cream into pan juices in the pot and cook over medium heat, whisking as the sauce reduces and thickens. Carve the bird, arrange on a platter, and spoon sauce over the chicken.

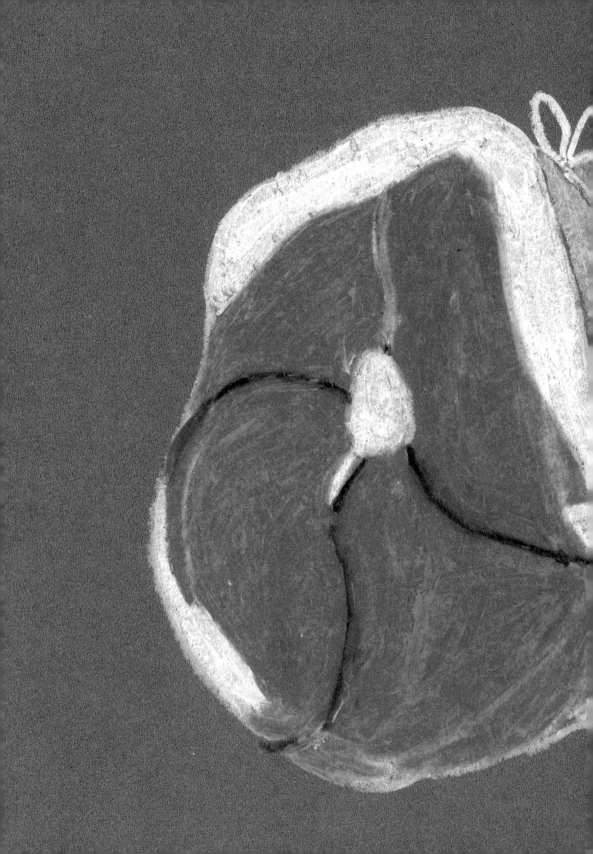

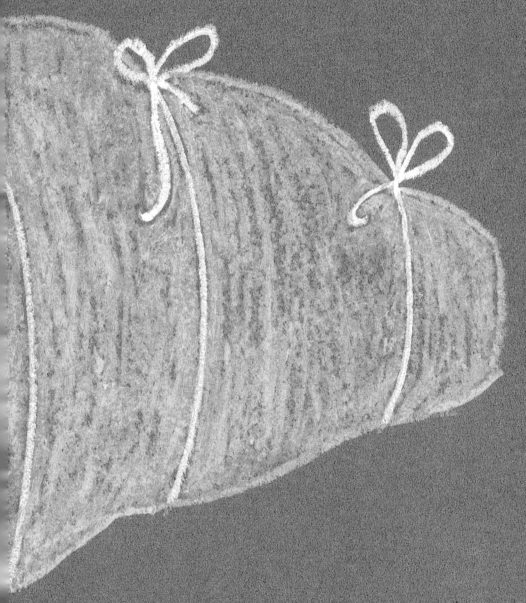

SERIOUS MEAT

FRESH HAM WITH MADEIRA SAUCE
serves 12

A fresh ham is really a leg of pork that hasn't been cured or smoked. You can either use the front, called a picnic ham, or the boned meaty sirloin half of a hind leg, which will give you prettier slices of meat. We ask our butcher to do the dirty work and remove the bone. We leave the skin on to protect the meat and keep it juicy. Low heat ensures moist meat, so cook it long and slow.

2 tablespoons finely chopped fresh sage leaves
½ nutmeg, grated
2 teaspoons Chinese five-spice powder

Salt and pepper
1 boned fresh ham, 8–10 pounds, skin intact
1 cup Madeira
1–2 tablespoons arrowroot

Preheat the oven to 200°. Mix together the sage, nutmeg, five-spice powder, and a good seasoning of salt and pepper in a small bowl. Rub meaty side of ham with the herb and spice mixture. The ham will be a rather untidy, lumpy piece of meat but when you tie it up it will be a neat package. Roll the meat into a compact shape and tie with kitchen string. Put in a roasting pan, skin side up, and cover with a lid or with aluminum foil. Cook in the oven until the meat is very tender, 6–8 hours.

Remove from the oven and transfer the roast to a cutting board and allow it to rest for 20–30 minutes. Pour the pan juices into a big glass measuring cup or a glass bowl. Use a spoon to remove all the fat.

You should have 2–3 cups of pan juices after you remove the fat. Pour the juices into a small pan and bring to a simmer over medium heat. Add the Madeira. Mix the arrowroot and 3 tablespoons water together in a little bowl. Add to the sauce and stir until it thickens. Add more arrowroot stirred into a little water if the sauce isn't thick enough. Don't allow the sauce to come to a boil or else it will thin out. Keep it just under a simmer.

Cut off and discard the skin and all but a thin layer of fat. Slice the meat and serve with the Madeira sauce.

Left: Roasted Pork Belly with Céléri Rémoulade, served with baked sweet potato; above: getting its second heating

ROASTED PORK BELLY
serves 6–8

We like to start with low heat and slowly cook the meat, then we increase the heat to crisp up the fat. If you can't find skin-on pork belly, don't worry. The belly's thick layer of fat will protect the tender meat as it cooks. And the skin— even though delicious—can be pretty chewy.

2 tablespoons kosher salt

2 tablespoons sugar

2 tablespoons fresh thyme leaves

2 teaspoons ground black pepper

3 pounds skin-on pork belly

1 cup apple cider

Mix together the salt, sugar, thyme, and pepper in a small bowl. Place the belly skin side up on a cutting board. Use a very, very sharp knife or (believe it or not) a matte knife to score through the tough skin and fat in a fine crosshatch pattern. (If you can't find skin-on pork belly just score through the fat with a sharp knife.) Rub the salt mixture on both sides of the meat. Put it in a large resealable bag and refrigerate for up to 24 hours. Rinse the meat in cold water. Dry well with a paper towels.

Preheat oven to 250°. Put the meat skin (or fat) side up in a roasting pan. Add the apple cider to the pan. Cover and roast for 1½ hours, basting occasionally. Increase the oven temperature to 400°. Roast until the meat is very tender, and the skin or fat is golden brown, about 1 hour.

Remove from the oven, and set aside to cool. Wrap in plastic or foil and place on a small baking sheet that just holds the meat. Place another baking sheet of the same size on top of the pork and weigh down with a few heavy cans. Refrigerate for several hours.

Preheat oven to 350°. Slice or cut in squares and reheat for about 20 minutes.

CÉLÉRI RÉMOULADE

Peel a 1-pound celery root then finely juilienne the flesh. Mix together the juice of 2 lemons, 2 tablespoons Dijon mustard, and ⅓–½ cup heavy cream in a large bowl. Add the celery root, mix together, and season with salt and pepper. —— *serves 6–8*

MOROCCAN LAMB ROAST

Sukey and John Jamison raise some of the most delicious lamb around on their farm in Latrobe, Pennsylvania. There the sheep gambol in bluegrass and nibble on white clover in the foothills of the Appalachians. We've been ordering their lamb for years. They have sent us every part—from chops to whole lambs for our lamb roasts. But our very favorite new cut is their mini-roast. It seems that people don't have time to roast a whole leg, and for chefs, (who buy much of their meat), a leg is tricky because it has so many different muscles in it, making each slice quite different from the next. So the Jamisons began to butcher whole legs into smaller cuts. The top round or topside mini-lamb roast, cut from the leg, usually weighs about 1½ pounds. It's one of the prettiest pieces of meat we've seen. The grain of the muscle all goes the same way so it is a breeze to slice. This cut usually shows up in Australia and New Zealand, where lamb is king, but is just showing up here.

Use whatever spices you like to make your own rub. We love Moroccan flavors with lamb.

Preheat the oven to 350°. Mix together 1 tablespoon ground cumin, 1 teaspoon ground coriander, 1 teaspoon ground cinnamon, 1 teaspoon ground cardamom and a big pinch of sugar in a small bowl. (Better yet, grind the whole seeds in a mortar and pestle or a spice grinder.) Season a topside mini-lamb roast all over with salt and pepper, then rub with the spice mixture. Heat 1 tablespoon olive oil in a heavy ovenproof skillet over medium-high heat. Brown the lamb on all sides, about 10 minutes, then put the skillet in the oven and cook for 20 minutes. Check the temperature with an instant-read thermometer. For medium-rare lamb it should read 120°. Remove from the oven and let it rest for 10 minutes. Slice the roast across the grain and serve with mint sauce. —— *serves 2–4*

MINT SAUCE

Mix together a large handful chopped fresh mint leaves, a small handful chopped fresh parsley leaves, 1 minced clove garlic, salt and pepper, juice of a lemon, and about ½ cup really good olive oil. Adjust the seasonings to your own taste. —— *makes about ½ cup*

BRAISED BEEF WITH CURRANTS & CARAWAY
serves 4–6

It may seem mad and extravagant to braise prime rib rather than a less expensive cut, but the meat is incomparably luxurious cooked this way. The flavors of this dish are reminiscent of sauerbraten—sweet and sour, fragrant and spicy. But there is an added richness from red wine instead of vinegar and prime meat instead of pot roast. And because the meat is so tender, you don't have to marinate it for three days. We like to serve this with slices of the very darkest rye bread slathered with butter.

4 ounces slab bacon, cut into
   very small cubes
4 yellow onions, halved lengthwise
1 clove garlic, finely minced
Salt and pepper
2 tablespoons caraway seeds

1 cup dried currants
2 cups red wine
1 prime rib of beef (2 ribs),
   4-pounds, first cut
1–2 teaspoons arrowroot

Preheat the oven to 200°. Sauté the bacon in a large heavy pot with a lid over medium-high heat. When the bacon has released some of its fat, place the onions, cut side down, in the pot. Add the garlic. Season to taste with salt and pepper. Scatter the caraway seeds and currants around the onions. Add the wine.

Season the roast all over with lots of salt and pepper. Place the meat, rib side down, on top of the onions. Cover, transfer to the oven, and cook until the meat is very tender, about 4 hours.

Remove the meat and onions from the pot, taking care to keep the onions intact. Remove any fat and slice the meat into pieces. Return the pot with the sauce to the top of the stove, and over medium heat, reduce the sauce by half. Dissolve the arrowroot in 2 tablespoons water in a small bowl, then using a wooden spoon, stir it into the sauce. Continue stirring as the sauce thickens. Don't allow it to come to a boil.

To serve, either return the meat and onions to the pot, or arrange them on a platter. Spoon the sauce, along with all the currants and caraway seeds, over the meat and onions.

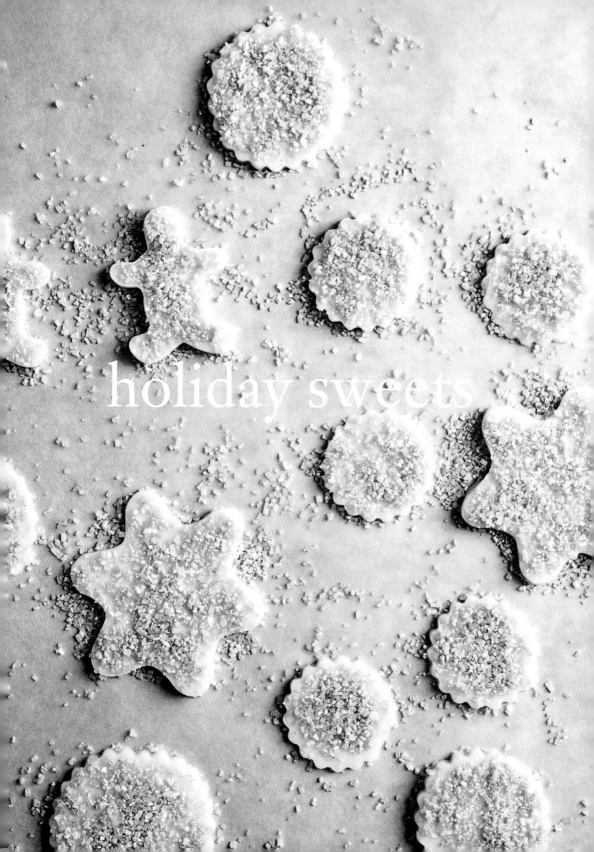

holiday sweets

SUGAR COOKIES
makes about 3 dozen

While poking around in a cookware store recently, we wandered into the baking section and came upon a handsome set of cookie cutters. They made us want to bake buttery little sugar cookies, which immediately made us think of our friend Katherine Yang. She is an exquisite baker whose pastries and desserts always balance sweet and savory perfectly—a quality we love because we're really not big dessert eaters. We bought the cookie cutters and gave Katherine a call. Ever gracious, and in fact delighted that we asked, she shared her recipe for these tender, subtly sophisticated cookies. Just the kind we had in mind.

Like most bakers, Katherine relies on measuring her ingredients by weight, not volume, for the most consistent results. We agree, but have included both methods below in case you don't have a scale. We found two other points in her meticulous notes that really did make a difference: letting the dough rest in the refrigerator, and making sure the dough is always cold when it's being worked. What's that expression?—God is in the details.

2 cups (284g) all-purpose flour
2 teaspoons (7g) kosher salt
1 large egg (50g)
1 large egg yolk (20g)
16 tablespoons (2 sticks) (227g) unsalted butter, at room temperature

½ cup (52g) powdered sugar, sifted
¼ cup (50g) granulated sugar
1 tablespoon (15g) vanilla bean paste or vanilla extract
Decorating sprinkles and sugars or other cookie decorations, optional

Sift the flour and salt together into a medium bowl and set aside. Lightly whisk together the whole egg and egg yolk in a small bowl and set aside.

Beat together the butter, powdered sugar, granulated sugar, and vanilla bean paste in a large mixing bowl with an electric mixer on medium speed until light and fluffy. Add the eggs and beat until just combined. Add the sifted flour and beat just until the dough is smooth.

Cut 8 pieces of parchment paper into 8"× 12" sheets. Lay one sheet on a flat work surface and put a quarter of the dough in the center. Lay another sheet on top of the dough then roll the dough out between the sheets until it is ¼–⅛ inch thick. Transfer the rolled-out dough to a flat tray. Repeat with the remaining dough, stacking the sheets of dough on top of each other on the tray. Cover with plastic wrap and refrigerate for at least 4 hours and up to 3 days.

Preheat the oven to 350°.

Take one sheet of dough out of the refrigerator at a time. Peel off the top sheet of parchment. Use a cookie cutter to cut out desired shapes, leaving them in place. Dust the cutter with a little flour if the dough begins to stick.

Using a thin spatula, transfer the cut out shapes to a parchment paper–lined baking sheet, spacing them about 2 inches apart. Decorate them, if you like, with decorating sprinkles and/or sugars. Refrigerate the cut-out shapes on the baking sheet until cold. Repeat until all of the dough has been cut into shapes. Refrigerate the dough whenever it becomes too soft to work with. Re-roll the scraps between sheets of parchment paper, refrigerate dough until firm, and repeat the process until all the dough has been cut out.

Bake the cookies, rotating the baking sheet halfway through baking, until they are slightly puffed and the edges are pale golden brown, 10–12 minutes. Remove the cookies from the oven and let cool for 5 minutes on the baking sheet, then transfer them to a wire rack to cool completely. The cookies will keep for up to 2 weeks in an airtight container.

COCONUT COOKIES ❈ Follow directions for making Sugar Cookies dough, substituting 1 teaspoon coconut extract for the vanilla.

LEMON COOKIES ❈ Follow directions for making Sugar Cookies dough, substituting 1 tablespoon freshly grated lemon zest and 2 teaspoons fresh lemon juice for the vanilla.

NUT COOKIES ❈ Follow directions for making Sugar Cookies dough. Sprinkle the tops of the cut-out dough with some chopped nuts before baking them. You'll need about ½ cup chopped nuts. Don't use toasted nuts; the raw nuts will toast while baking.

ORANGE-ROSEMARY COOKIES ❈ Follow directions for making Sugar Cookies dough, substituting freshly grated zest of 2 oranges (1½–2 tablespoons) and 1 tablespoon finely minced fresh rosemary leaves for the vanilla.

Overleaf: left, cookie cutter shapes in rolled-out dough; right, unbaked cookies ready to go in the oven

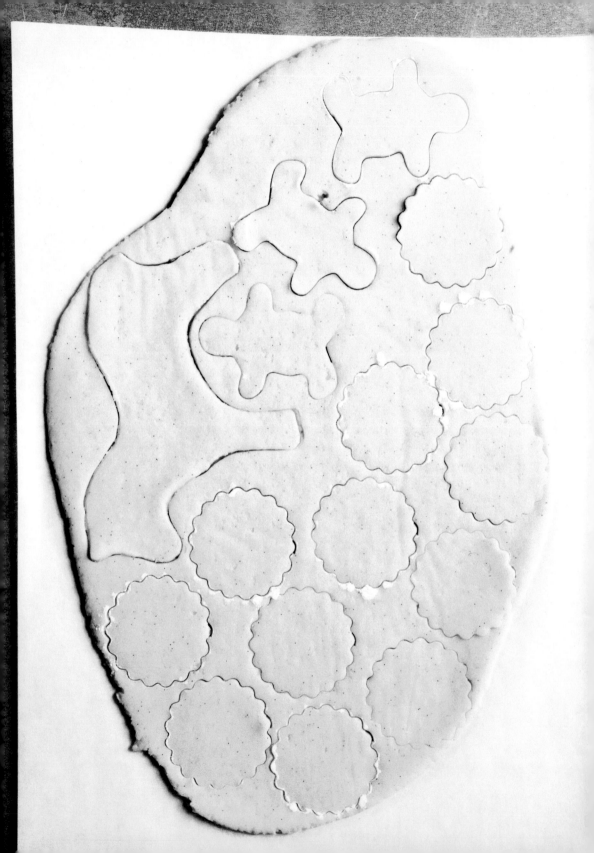

OEUFS À LA NEIGE
serves 8–10

It's hard to be spectacular and cozy at the same time but this classic does just that. Drizzle on the caramel just before serving so that it won't melt.

FOR THE CRÈME ANGLAISE
3 cups whole milk
¼ cup granulated sugar
1 vanilla bean, slit lengthwise
6 egg yolks

FOR THE MERINGUES
6 egg whites
¼ teaspoon cream of tartar
¾ cup superfine sugar

FOR THE CARAMEL
½ cup granulated sugar

For the crème anglaise, put the milk, sugar, and vanilla bean in a medium pot and bring just to a simmer over medium heat. Remove from the heat. Whisk the egg yolks together in a large bowl until just mixed. Whisk the hot milk into the yolks ½ cup at a time. Return the milk to the pot and cook over low heat, stirring constantly with a wooden spoon, until the sauce thickens, about 20 minutes. Don't let it boil. Strain through a sieve into a bowl. Set aside to cool.

For the meringues, bring 2 large shallow pans of water to just below a simmer over low heat. Beat the egg whites and cream of tartar with an electric mixer on medium speed until frothy, increase the speed to high, and beat until the whites form stiff peaks. Continue beating, gradually adding the sugar, until the meringue is very stiff and glossy.

Use a 4-ounce ice-cream scoop to form meringue eggs, gently dropping them into the water as you go. Poach 5 to 6 at a time per pan (they expand), keeping the water just below a simmer. Poach for 4–5 minutes, then gently turn over, using a slotted spoon, and poach for another 4–5 minutes. The meringue is set when it has the firmness of a poached egg. Transfer with a slotted spoon to a clean dish towel. They can rest a few hours, unrefrigerated, until ready to serve.

Just before serving, pour the crème anglaise into a deep serving platter. "Float" the meringues in the sauce.

For the caramel, shortly before serving, heat the sugar and ¼ cup water in a small, heavy saucepan over medium-high heat. Swirl the pan until the sugar turns into a pale caramel syrup. Remove immediately from heat. The caramel will continue to cook and darken off the heat. Use a fork to drizzle threads of caramel over the meringues.

PETS DE NONNES
(Nuns' Farts)
makes about 3 dozen

We first had these sweet little puffs at Restaurant Daniel in New York. Toward the end of a delicious meal, a waiter arrived at the table with a napkined plate piled high with sugary puffs. "Would you care for a nun's fart?", he asked with a hint of a smile, "Compliments of the chef". They were heavenly indeed!

FOR THE PUFFS
6 tablespoons butter
Pinch salt
1 cup sifted all-purpose flour
4 eggs

Canola oil

FOR THE ORANGE SUGAR
1 cup sugar
Grated zest of 1 orange

For the puffs, put the butter, salt, and 1 cup water in a medium-sized heavy pot and bring to a boil over medium-high heat. Remove the pot from the heat and add the flour all at once, stirring with a wooden spoon until the batter all comes together and pulls away from the sides of the pot in a mass. Reduce the heat to low, and return the pot to the heat. Stir for a minute to dry out the dough. Remove the pot from the heat.

Beat in the eggs one at a time, fully incorporating each one into the dough before adding the next. The dough may look a little slippery but just continue to beat with the wooden spoon and it will absorb the egg and all come together.

For the orange sugar, mix the sugar and the orange zest together in a bowl and set aside.

Add oil to a wide pot to reach a depth of about 2 inches. Heat the oil over medium-high heat until the temperature is 275°. (Use a candy thermometer if you have one, or dip a wooden chopstick in the oil to the bottom of the pot. If a steady stream of bubbles float up from the tip, the oil is ready—no bubbles, too cold; vigorous bubbles, too hot.) Drop dough by the tablespoon (don't crowd the pot) into the hot oil and cook, turning them over as they brown, for about 5 minutes. Use a wire skimmer or slotted spatula to transfer the puffs to a wire rack. Roll them in the orange sugar and serve.

PEAR UPSIDE-DOWN CAKE
makes one 9-inch cake

This simple cake, full of warm ginger flavor, relies on voluptuous pears that are ripe and juicy. Two common varieties, Bartlett and Anjou, are good choices.

6 tablespoons unsalted butter

⅓ cup dark brown sugar

1 pinch plus ¼ teaspoon salt

3 ripe pears

1 cup all-purpose flour

2 teaspoons ground ginger

1 teaspoon baking powder

½ cup whole milk

2 eggs

1 cup granulated sugar

1 teaspoon vanilla bean paste or vanilla extract

Preheat the oven to 375°. Melt 4 tablespoons of the butter in a small saucepan over low heat. Add the dark brown sugar and a pinch of salt and stir until well combined. Pour the brown sugar mixture into a 9-inch round cake pan, spreading it out to cover the bottom of the pan; set aside.

Peel and halve the pears. Use a small spoon (a teaspoon from a measuring set works well) to scoop out the core, then use a paring knife to notch out the stem. Arrange the pears cut side up around the bottom of the prepared pan.

Wisk together the flour, ginger, baking powder, and ¼ teaspoon salt in a small bowl; set aside. Bring the milk almost to a boil in a small pan over medium heat. Add the remaining 2 tablespoons butter. Keep hot over low heat.

Beat the eggs in a mixing bowl with an electric mixer on medium-high speed until thick and pale, about 3 minutes. Gradually add the granulated sugar, beating constantly for about 5 minutes. Add the flour mixture and stir well. Add the vanilla and the hot milk, stirring until the batter is smooth. Pour the batter over the pears.

Bake the cake until golden, and a wooden skewer comes out clean when inserted in the center, about 40 minutes. Let the cake cool for about 10 minutes, then invert it onto a serving plate, fruit side up. Serve the cake slightly warm or at room temperature.

APPLE FRITTERS
makes about 2½ dozen

We consider ourselves pretty resourceful cooks when necessary, never too reliant on anything beyond some good, basic kitchen tools—a couple of knives, a vegetable peeler, a mortar and pestle. But our ingenuity even surprised us the time we were making these fritters without an apple corer and used a metal screw cap from a wine bottle to cut out the core and make nice round holes in the center of the apple slices. A cork just wouldn't have cut it!

Our fritter batter, unlike many that use egg and some type of leavening, is essentially a thicker version of the one we use for making fritto misto. We like the way its lacy, crisp, less cakey coating, lets the apple flavor shine through.

1 cup all-purpose flour
½ teaspoon salt
1½ cups hard cider, beer, Prosecco, or club soda

4 sweet, crisp apples
1 lemon, halved
Canola or corn oil
Powdered sugar

Whisk the flour and salt together in a medium bowl. Gradually add the hard cider, whisking it in little by little until the batter is thick enough to coat the apple slices, a bit thinner than pancake batter and thicker than heavy cream. (You may not need to use all the liquid.) Set batter aside.

Peel the apples and use an apple corer to remove the center. Slice the apples crosswise into ¼-inch-thick rings. Squeeze some of the juice from the lemon over the apples as you work to keep them from turning brown.

Add oil to a heavy skillet to reach a depth of 1 inch. Heat the oil over medium-high heat until the temperature is 350°. (Use a candy thermometer or dip a wooden chopstick in the oil to the bottom of the skillet. If a steady stream of bubbles float up from the tip, the oil is ready—no bubbles, too cold; vigorous bubbles, too hot.)

Pat the apple slices dry with paper towels. Working in small batches, dip each slice into the batter, coating it completely, then slip it into the hot oil. Deep-fry the fritters, turning them once or twice for even browning, until puffed and pale golden, 3–5 minutes. Use a wire skimmer or slotted spatula to transfer the fritters to a wire rack. Dust the fritters with powdered sugar and serve hot.

OUR BOOKS

This is the fifth book of our recipe collections—Canal House Cooking. We publish three seasonal volumes a year, each filled with delicious recipes for you from us. To sign up for a subscription or to buy books, visit thecanalhouse.com.

OUR WEBSITE

Our website, thecanalhouse.com, a companion to this book, offers our readers ways to get the best from supermarkets (what and how to buy, how to store it, cook it, and serve it). We'll tell you why a certain cut of meat works for a particular recipe, which boxes, cans, bottles, or tins are worthwhile; which apples are best for baking; and what to look for when buying olive oil, salt, or butter. We'll also suggest what's worth seeking out from specialty stores or mail-order sources and why. And wait, there's more. We share our stories, the wines we are drinking, gardening tips, and events; and our favorite books, cooks, and restaurants are on our site—take a look.

RUSS & DAUGHTERS
CAVIAR

CAVIAR

MALOSSOL CAVIAR

CASPI

MALOSS

CASPI

Product of USSR - To be weighed at time

CAV

L CAVIAR